The Heart of the Old Testament

second edition

Other Works by Ronald Youngblood

The Amarna Correspondence of Rib-Haddi,
Prince of Byblos
The Book of Genesis: An Introductory Commentary
The Book of Isaiah: An Introductory Commentary
Evangelicals and Inerrancy (editor)
Exodus
Faith of Our Fathers
1–2 Samuel *(Expositor's Bible Commentary)*
The Genesis Debate: Persistent Questions about Creation
and the Flood (editor)
How It All Began
Nelson's Comfort Print Bible Concordance
Nelson's New Illustrated Bible Dictionary (gen. ed.)
Nelson's Quick Reference Bible Concordance
The New Compact Key Reference Concordance
Special Day Sermons, 2d ed.
Themes from Isaiah
A Tribute to Gleason Archer (coeditor)

The Heart of the Old Testament

second edition

A Survey of Key Theological Themes

Ronald Youngblood

Baker Books

A Division of Baker Book House Co
Grand Rapids, Michigan 49516

© 1998 by Ronald Youngblood

Published by Baker Books
a division of Baker Publishing Group
P.O. Box 6287, Grand Rapids, MI 49516-6287
www.bakerbooks.com

Originally published in 1968 by Harvest Publications under the title *Great Themes of the Old Testament.*

First Baker edition published 1971.

Eighth printing, December 2005

Printed in the United States of America

Library of Congress Cataloging-in-Publication Data
Youngblood, Ronald F.
   The heart of the Old Testament : a survey of key theological themes / Ronald
Youngblood. — 2nd ed.
      p.   -cm.
   Includes bibliographical references and indexes.
   ISBN 0-8010-2172-3 (pbk.)
   1. Bible. O.T.—Theology. I. Title.
BS1192.5.Y65   1998
221.6′6—dc21   98-17841

Unless otherwise indicated, all Scripture quotations are taken from the Holy Bible, New International Version. Copyright © 1973, 1978, 1984 by International Bible Society. Used by permission of Zondervan Bible Publishers.

Contents

Preface

The unity of the Bible has made an indelible impression on the minds and hearts of untold numbers of its readers. Not only does the subject matter of the first three chapters of Genesis bear a remarkable resemblance to that of the last three chapters of Revelation, but also all the chapters in between are so intimately interrelated as to betray the divine purpose that brought them into being. One means by which to demonstrate the basic oneness of the Scriptures is to trace the development of certain key ideas from one end of the Bible to the other. The purpose of this book is to do just that with nine of the themes that constitute the heart of the Old Testament.

In the pursuit of our goal we have attempted in each case to define the concept, describe the cultural setting in which it arose in ancient Israel, delineate the various stages through which God's people passed as they grew in their understanding of it, and discuss briefly its ultimate fulfillment in Jesus Christ. By so doing we earnestly hope that we shall help our readers to see more clearly the fact that the Word of God is essentially one Book.

The bibliography after the final chapter is intended to be representative rather than exhaustive. It would be impossible to express here the debt we owe to all who have taught us, whether in oral or written form, various aspects of the ideas treated in this volume. But we wish to give special thanks to Janice Raymond, who compliled the two indexes at the end of the book. And we are most grateful of all to the God who is the source and sustainer of every theme contained in Scripture. It is therefore to his glory that we dedicate the following pages.

1 Monotheism

I am God, and there is no other.

Isaiah 45:22

Until fairly recently, a few theologians were telling us that God was dead. These so-called Christian atheists did not always agree in their explanations of what it meant to say, "God is dead." Some of them felt that God died when Christ came to earth nearly two thousand years ago. Others stated that God had died within our own lifetime. Still others insisted that, although God may very well have been alive somewhere, for all practical purposes he had died because we had refused him entrance into our hearts and denied him relevance in our conduct and experience.

Needless to say, the true Christian could never deny the existence of God in theory and ought never to deny the relevance of God in practice. Of Jesus Christ, the Son of God, we often sing, "You ask me how I know he lives? He lives within my heart." And if we really know God the Son, we know God the Father also (John 14:7). It is highly unlikely that the temptation to "Christian atheism," which is in itself a contradiction in terms, could ever seriously affect the person who has been born again by God the Holy Spirit.

Similarly, the temptation to atheism was not a serious problem for believing Israelites in ancient times. They were convinced that only an immoral reprobate would be so foolish as to deny the existence of a supreme being (Ps. 14:1; 53:1). For the people of God in the Old Testament period, practicing the presence of God was life itself. Having respect for the Lord and holding him in awe was for them the very basis of knowledge and wisdom (Prov. 1:7; 9:10).

However, other temptations concerning the nature of God tantalized the people of ancient Israel. If they did not doubt the fact that there was at least one God, their neighbors from other nations often faced them with the possibility that there might be *more* than one. Egypt, for example, was a polytheistic nation. Its people believed and taught that there were many gods. In fact, they were convinced that their pharaoh himself was a god. Many of Israel's nearer neighbors, among them Edom and Moab, were henotheistic or monolatrous. They believed in and worshiped only one primary god, but they did not deny the existence of other secondary gods and goddesses. One of the questions that the Old Testament poses is whether the people of Israel would remain true to the God of their fathers—the God of Abraham, Isaac, and Jacob, the Creator and Lord of the universe. Would they maintain their belief in monotheism, or would they be attracted to monolatry, or henotheism, or—worst of all—polytheism?

Many students of comparative religion have taught that monotheism is a product of evolution. As human beings evolved, they have said, so also did their religions evolve from lower stages to ever higher stages, finally arriving at monotheism, the highest stage of all, the stage that proclaims the truth that there is only one God. Since Israel is a part of the human race, the Israelite religion must have begun, we are told, in the dim and distant past as animism, which teaches that all natural objects, whether animate or inanimate, are alive and indwelt by one or more supernatural spirits. From animism the idea developed in Israel that certain spirits are more powerful than others and therefore deserve to be called "gods." Among these would be the sun-god, the ocean-god, the river-god, the bull-god, and many similar deities. Thus, we are told, Israel became polytheistic. Eventually the *most* powerful of Israel's gods assumed his place of prominence above the others, and the people became henotheistic (believing in his supreme authority) and monolatrous (worshiping him alone). Finally, it is supposed, Israel reached the point of admitting that the lesser gods did not even exist and that in fact there was only one God. Comparative religion often teaches, then, that the religion of Israel underwent a process of evolution from animism to polytheism to henotheism to monotheism.

But it simply cannot be shown that there is a universal tendency on the part of polytheistic religions to gradually reduce the number of deities until finally arriving at only one deity. Indeed, in some instances such a religion may even add *more* deities as its adherents become aware of more and more natural phenomena to deify. At any rate the Old Testament teaches that monotheism, far from having evolved through the centuries of Israel's history, is one of the inspired insights revealed to the covenant people by the one true God himself.

The pure form of monotheism described in the Old Testament is unique to biblical religion. The God of the Old Testament is the transcendent Creator of everything that exists. He stands outside the universe; he is not a part of it. There are only three religions in our modern world that share this viewpoint, and all of them are based on the revealed religion of Israel. Judaism, in accepting the Old Testament as its Scriptures, has joyously affirmed the Old Testament view of God as well. The opening statement of its basic creed, known as the *Shema*, begins with the well-known words of Deuteronomy 6:4: "Hear, O Israel: The LORD our God, the LORD is one." In a similar way Christianity has confessed the same truth because Christ himself declared it to be a part of the most important commandment (Mark 12:28–30). Paul in fact defined monotheism in its most classic form in 1 Timothy 2:5: "There is one God." As the third major religion of our time that has embraced a transcendent form of monotheism, Islam has expressed the doctrine in the same clear-cut and categorical way. Five times a day the Muslim *muezzin* mounts his minaret and in a loud voice calls the faithful to prayer: "There is no god but God."

Certain other modern religions, such as Zoroastrianism and Sikhism, embrace forms of monotheism that are inferior to the Old Testament teaching. They are derived from earlier dualistic or polytheistic systems. Moreover they suggest that God is a part of this world order and not separate from it, and this by necessity rather than by choice. But only the religion of the Old Testament and its derivatives proclaim the one true God who is transcendent by nature and who is at the same time immanent by choice and condescension and grace. Only in such a context do we find statements like this: "For this is what the high and lofty One says—he who lives forever, whose name is holy: 'I live in a high and holy place, but also with him who is contrite and lowly in spirit' " (Isa. 57:15).

The monotheistic ideals of Israel's religion characterized it from the earliest days. Israel's Creator God is portrayed in majestic grandeur in the very first verse of Genesis. His existence is assumed rather than argued. He is placed outside the universe and above it as its Creator. The view of God taught by the first chapter of Genesis is opposed to an entire phalanx of false philosophies. Against materialism, which teaches that matter is everything and that it is eternal, Genesis 1 teaches that God is eternal, above matter, and the Creator of matter (which is therefore *neither* eternal *nor* everything). Against pantheism, which teaches that everything is God or gods, or that God is (or gods are) *in* everything, Genesis 1 teaches that God is *separate* from his creation and that he is *above* it. Against dualism, which teaches that there is a continuing struggle taking place between two more or less equally matched gods or principles, one evil and the other good, Genesis 1 posits one good God who in sequence declares his creative works to be "good" (Gen. 1:4, 9,

12, 18, 21, 25) and concludes by stamping the whole creative week "very good" (1:31). Against polytheism, which teaches that there are many gods who are often at odds with one another, Genesis 1 declares that there is only one beneficent God. No one can doubt that one of the great themes of the Old Testament is its pure, pervasive, unyielding monotheism.

It is also clear, however, that other alternatives competed for the attention and allegiance of God's children in ancient times. The teachings of the Near Eastern nature religions made their influence felt on the backgrounds and spiritual struggles of the Hebrew people even before the patriarchal period. Joshua 24:2 demonstrates that the ancestors of Abraham were polytheists. Abraham's Aramean relatives continued to keep statues of deities in their homes, a practice that Jacob's wife Rachel apparently approved of at one time (Gen. 31:17–35). Jacob himself found it necessary on one occasion to say to his household and to all who were with him, "Get rid of the foreign gods you have with you, and purify yourselves" (35:2). Indeed, we have no way of knowing whether Abraham himself, the patriarch who is considered by each of the three monotheistic religions previously mentioned to be its founder, was himself a thoroughgoing monotheist. That he was a *practical* monotheist cannot be denied. God monopolized Abraham to the extent that he had neither time nor room for competing deities, whether real or imaginary. But Abraham's own personal inclinations may well have been henotheistic rather than monotheistic, because nowhere in the Book of Genesis does he clearly deny the existence of other gods.

Moses is generally believed to be the father of Israelite monotheism. This does not mean that no Israelites were monotheists before him, nor does it mean that all Israelites would be monotheists after him. It simply means that Moses was the first, under the inspiration of the Holy Spirit, to define the nature of God in a clearly monotheistic way. The monotheistic background of Genesis 1 is in full agreement with such statements of Moses as we find in Deuteronomy 4:35, 39: "The LORD is God;

besides him there is no other. . . . The LORD is God in heaven above and on the earth below. There is no other." The first of the Ten Commandments, "You shall have no other gods before me" (Exod. 20:3; Deut. 5:7), deals with the temptation to succumb to henotheism or polytheism, a temptation that was a source of constant danger to the Israelites of the Old Testament period down to the time of the exile. The commandment is firm in its insistence that Israel is to have only one object of worship and allegiance: the one true God, the Lord God Almighty.

James Henry Breasted, a great Egyptologist of a former generation, referred to Pharaoh Amunhotep IV, also known as Akhenaten, as the first monotheist in history. It is certainly true that Akhenaten and his family abandoned Egyptian polytheism and worshiped only the sun-disk Aten as the source of all life. But we should also observe that Akhenaten did not deny to his courtiers the questionable privilege of worshiping him as the deified pharaoh. As for the rest of the Egyptian population, they remained either ignorant of or antagonistic toward the new religion that Akhenaten had instituted. We must also note that this so-called monotheism was neither more nor less than sun-worship.

Nevertheless, it is intriguing to speculate as to whether the religion of Akhenaten and Mosaic monotheism are related in any way. If the scholars who believe that the exodus of the Israelites from Egypt occurred in about 1290 B.C. are correct, the boy Moses would have lived in the court of Akhenaten, who ruled over Egypt from about 1377 to about 1361 B.C. It would therefore be possible to look upon the pharaonic religion of this period as a degraded form of the monotheism of Moses. Another option would be to view Mosaic monotheism as a divinely inspired and revealed reaction against the crudities and absurdities of Akhenaten's faith. In any event, if Moses and Akhenaten were contemporaries they could hardly have avoided discussing together the nature of God, a subject that was so significant in the lives of both of them.

During another critical period in Israel's history, a contest took place on Mount Carmel between Elijah on the one hand and the "four hundred and fifty prophets of Baal and the four hundred prophets of Asherah" (1 Kings 18:19) on the other. It soon became evident, however, that the real contest was between the God of Elijah and the Baal of Jezebel. Elijah challenged the false prophets with this ultimatum: "You call on the name of your god, and I will call on the name of the LORD. The god who answers by fire— he is God" (18:24). The climax of the story leaves no doubt that Baal was no match for the living God whom Elijah served.

But the results of the contest on Mount Carmel were soon forgotten, and the writing prophets from the eighth century B.C. and onward found it necessary to remind their people again and again of the vast gulf that separated the one true God from the idols of his imaginary pagan counterparts. The common noun *baal* means simply "master" or "husband." But to avoid all possibility of misunderstanding, the people of Israel were never to refer to the Lord as "my Baal" (Hos. 2:16). The prophets ridiculed idolatry as foolish worship of inanimate objects (4:12; Isa. 2:8; 17:8; 31:7; 44:19; Hab. 2:18–19). Such false gods lack entirely the personal dimension that characterizes genuine deity.

It is true that sometimes the prophets seem to ascribe to pagan gods actions that are appropriate only to living beings. For example, Isaiah tells us that when the Lord comes to Egypt "the idols of Egypt tremble before him" (Isa. 19:1). Later, Jeremiah says concerning the gods of Babylonia that "Bel will be put to shame, Marduk filled with terror. Her images will be put to shame and her idols filled with terror" (Jer. 50:2). Whether we are to understand such statements in a figurative way or whether we are to interpret them as referring to demonic activity underlying false worship is difficult to say. Perhaps there is an element of truth in both explanations. In any case, the contrast between dead idols and the living God is brought into sharp relief in such passages as the following: "Like a scarecrow in a melon patch, their idols cannot speak; they must be carried because they cannot walk. Do not fear them; they can do no harm nor can they do any good. . . . But the LORD is the true God; he is the living God, the eternal King. When he is angry, the earth trembles; the nations cannot endure his wrath" (10:5, 10).

All the evidence we have leads us to believe that after the destruction of Jerusalem and Solomon's temple in 586 B.C. the people of Judah were rarely if ever tempted by idolatry. Judah had experienced severe retribution; it would now experience sincere repentance. The people knew they were being punished for their sins, and the sight of the excessive polytheism of Babylonia was revolting to the exiled remnant and helped to make the Jews a truly monotheistic people from that day to this. Judaism today gladly shares with Christianity the divine affirmation of the Scriptures: "This is what the LORD . . . says: 'I am the LORD, and there is no other. . . . And there is no other god apart from me, a righteous God and a Savior; there is none but me' " (Isa. 45:18, 21). Since the sixth century B.C. observant Jews have been thoroughly and uncompromisingly monotheistic.

This fact helps to explain why the Jews of Jesus' time found it so difficult to accept his messianic claims. He said that he was God's Son, and such statements seemed blasphemous and worthy of death to his monotheistic countrymen (John 8:48–59; 10:22–39). But the doctrine of the deity of Christ is not at all incompatible with the highest form of monotheism. In fact, hints pointing to a plurality within the personality of God are to be found already in the Old Testament itself. In addition to the Father, the Spirit and the Word were active in creation from the beginning (Gen. 1:1–3), and the Word is none other than Jesus Christ (John 1:1–14). We must allow for progressive revelation as God discloses to us, step by step, his nature and purposes (Heb. 1:1–2). That God is one is a doctrine enunciated clearly and frequently in the Old Testament. That God is three in one is a doctrine that is merely foreshadowed by the Old Testament and that does not burst forth into the clear light of revelation until New Testament times (Matt. 28:19; 2 Cor. 13:14).

Often mentioned in connection with Old Testament prefigurations of the uniplurality of God is the manifestation of his being that is known as the "angel of God" or the "angel of the Lord." Interpreters differ widely in their understanding of this divine messenger. Some feel that he was an angel, a finite spirit who executed the commands of God and who was in subjection to God. Others insist that he was a manifestation of God who became a creature, one in essence with God while at the same time becoming different from him, a kind of preincarnate appearance of the Second Person of the Godhead.

While it is difficult to decide between these two views and their various modifications, of which there are many, a fact that has come to the fore in recent years may be of some help. In ancient times a messenger of a royal court carried with him all the credentials of the king himself when he was dispatched on an imperial mission. His personality, his attributes, his commands, while remaining his own, were also the king's. The royal messenger represented the royal person in every respect. Whereas this may be a poor illustration of the matter at issue, in a similar way the angel of God could refer to God as his sender, and at the same time he could speak as though he himself were God. In such a way the angel of God foreshadowed the uniplurality of the divine nature in the Old Testament period.

At any rate, God did not reveal himself prematurely in clearly defined trinitarian terms in the Old Testament Scriptures. To have done so would have been to provide needless temptations to polytheism in light of the cultures of that early time. The deity of the Messiah and the personality of the Holy Spirit were thus kept in the background of Old Testament teaching. On the other hand, although the New Testament writers clearly affirmed trinitarianism, they did not shrink from teaching monotheistic doctrine as well. For them, no conflict existed between the two ideas. Paul's sermon to the men of Athens is thoroughly monotheistic (Acts 17:22–31), and to the church at Corinth he stated in no uncertain terms that "there is no God but one" (1 Cor. 8:4). On the latter occasion he hastened to add, however, by using a partial trinitarian formula, that "for us there is but one God, the Father, from whom all things came and for whom we live; and there is but one Lord, Jesus Christ, through whom all things came and through whom we live" (8:6). So also we as Christians today joyfully confess, as trinitarian monotheists, that God is one and that he is also three in one.

2

Sovereignty

The LORD does whatever pleases him.
Psalm 135:6

In a devastatingly frank Old Testament passage, false gods and the nations who worship them are described as follows: "Their idols are silver and gold, made by the hands of men. They have mouths, but cannot speak, eyes, but they cannot see; they have ears, but cannot hear, noses, but they cannot smell; they have hands, but cannot feel, feet, but they cannot walk; nor can they utter a sound with their throats. Those who make them will be like them, and so will all who trust in them" (Ps. 115:4–8).

By way of contrast, the psalmist introduces the passage with this portrayal of the true and living God: "Our God is in heaven; he does whatever pleases him" (115:3). As Israelite believers could refer to the nature of their God only in terms of monotheism, so also could they refer to the purposes of their God only in terms of sovereignty. God, for ancient Israel, was supreme in power and superior in position to all other so-called gods that might claim the allegiance of his people. As the Creator of the universe, he was independent of it and unlimited by it. His authority was original and unconditioned, and his jurisdiction over everything and everyone was free and unfettered. He was the only God, and he was the only Sovereign.

As one of the great themes close to the heart of the Old Testament, the sovereignty of God needs to be reaffirmed by people individually and collectively in our own day. If the deification of a man—however powerful he might be—was a temptation to the pharaohs of ancient Egypt, the humanization of God is no less tantalizing a tendency in our modern scientific age. Current patronizing references to God are appalling and blasphemous, to say the least. To call God "the man upstairs" or "the someone up there who likes me" is to display a deplorable lack of understanding concerning his nature. When recently asked for her opinion of God, a young lady answered typically, "Oh, I like him all right, but I'm not crazy about him." Such statements are symptomatic of the modern tendency to reduce the Creator to the level of the creature, to reconstruct God in our own image, to make human beings the standard and judge of all that exists, and thus to deny the very possibility of the sovereignty of God. Such statements are a far cry from the exalted view implied in definitions of God like that of the Westminster Catechism: "God is a Spirit, infinite, eternal, and unchangeable, in his being, wisdom, power, holiness, justice, goodness, and truth."

The above-cited definition, which is scriptural and therefore solidly based, leads inevitably to the conclusion that God is sovereign over all. It is perhaps best to exclude his sovereignty from the list of his attributes and to affirm instead that it arises out of them. God is sovereign because of his attributes. His characteristics in all their perfection form the foundation of his sovereign dominion over the universe.

The very word *God* itself leads to a similar conclusion. Among the ancient Semites the common noun for *god*, a word shared by the Hebrew people with their neighbors, was *el*, as in *beth-el*, "House of God." But the word *el* was also used sometimes in the Old Testament in the impersonal sense of "power" or "strength." Particularly instructive in this connection is Proverbs 3:27: "Do not withhold good from those who deserve it, when it is in your power [*el*] to act." It is clear that *el* in this context involves not only power but also the prerogative to decide whether and when and how to use it.

As the only true *el* that the Old Testament knows, God is sovereign omnipotence par excellence. In ancient times a person's name was equivalent to his or her personality or character or history. Typical of this concept is the statement of Abigail to David in 1 Samuel 25:25: "May my lord pay no attention to that wicked man Nabal. He is just like his name—his name is Fool, and folly goes with him." The fact that the Hebrew word *nabal* means "fool" clarifies Abigail's sarcasm. The identification of name with personality also helps us to understand why the names of several biblical personages were changed at crucial times in their lives. It was believed that changing a man's name signalized a corresponding change in his character. Such a belief achieved divinely ordained actuality when Abram became Abraham ("Father of Many," Gen. 17:5), when Jacob became Israel ("He Struggles with God," 32:28), and when Simon became Peter ("Rock," Matt. 16:18).

Such examples illustrate for us the great truth that God's name, *El,* proclaims his character as the all-powerful and sovereign Lord of the universe. He is just like his name. His attributes and his name demonstrate his sovereignty. But we have not exhausted the basis of God's sovereignty by speaking merely of his name and his characteristics. After all, sovereignty is a term of relationship. Over what—or whom—is our God sovereign?

To begin with, he is, as we have already indicated, the Lord of the universe. The verb *create* in the Old Testament has only and always God as its subject; human beings never create anything. The first verse of Genesis tells us that "God created the heavens and the earth." The Bible describes for us the God who, as the Creator of the universe, is also its absolute proprietor. He who made it and sustains it also owns it and has the privilege of disposing of it as he desires. No one can dispute his authority in this regard because, as he himself has told us, "Before me no god was formed, nor will there be one after me" (Isa. 43:10). His relationship to the universe is clearly one of undisputed sovereignty.

In Genesis 1:21 we meet the second biblical occurrence of the verb *create:* "God created the great creatures of the sea and every living and moving thing." God's sovereignty here relates to his creation of and lordship over animate life. It is almost an understatement to assert that God is innately and infinitely superior to all of his creatures, and it is not difficult to see why there was no room in Israel's faith for the grotesque worship of animals or animal-headed deities so characteristic of other ancient religious practice.

There is no more solemn statement in all of Scripture referring to the relationship between God and humankind than that in Genesis 1:27, an exquisite little poem in which we find the third biblical occurrence of the verb *create,* three times repeated: "God created man in his own image, in the image of God he created him; male and female he created them." Our creatureliness at the hands of an all-wise Creator should temper our tendency to complain about the circumstances in which we sometimes find ourselves. The Bible looks at criticism of this kind as though it were leveled against God himself: "You turn things upside down, as if the potter were thought to be like the clay! Shall what is formed say of him who formed it, 'He did not make me'? Can the pot say of the potter, 'He knows nothing'?" (Isa. 29:16). In view of our sinfulness and our resultant forfeiture of all claims on the mercy of God, we should rather rejoice in God's sovereignty over our lives in the words of Isaiah 64:8: "O LORD, you are our Father. We are the clay, you are the potter; we are all the work of your hand."

So the Genesis creation story may serve as a worthy introduction to the subject of the characteristics of God's sovereignty, because it teaches us that his dominion is universal. None of his creatures, from the highest to the lowest, is excluded from it. David's prayer in 1 Chronicles 29, of which the Lord's Prayer is strikingly reminiscent, extols the universal extent of the sovereignty of God: "Everything in heaven and earth is yours. Yours, O LORD, is the kingdom; you are exalted as head over all" (29:11). In a similar way two of the nature hymns attributed to

David, Psalms 19 and 24, peal forth the praises of the God whose glory and handiwork the skies proclaim and who possesses the world and all who live in it.

The Scriptures also stress the absolute nature of God's sovereignty. Nothing in the universe can limit his authority or thwart his purposes, as even the pagan King Nebuchadnezzar of Babylonia affirmed: "He does as he pleases with the powers of heaven and the peoples of the earth. No one can hold back his hand or say to him: 'What have you done?' " (Dan. 4:35). Paul may have had in mind the fact that the sovereignty of God is not to be denied even in the innermost life of the believer when he assured his Christian readers that "it is God who works in you to will and to act according to his good purpose" (Phil. 2:13).

It hardly needs to be stressed that God's sovereignty is unchangeable (Mal. 3:6). The Lord of the universe will not swerve from his determined course of action. His dominion and authority may be ignored or rejected only at the peril of the offender. As the laws of nature control the physical universe, so also does the sovereignty of God bend his creatures to perform his will. The consequences are serious indeed for all who refuse to kneel before their Creator: "Woe to him who quarrels with his Maker, to him who is but a potsherd among the potsherds on the ground. Does the clay say to the potter, 'What are you making?' Does your work say, 'He has no hands'?" (Isa. 45:9).

One of the most instructive passages dealing with the subject of God's sovereignty is Paul's philosophy of history as he describes it in Acts 17:22–31. From it we learn of several ways in which God exercises his sovereignty in the universe and among his creatures. As the moral governor of his creation, he has established the spiritual and ethical rules by which he expects his children to conduct themselves (17:30–31). In our day much attention is being given to what is variously called "situation ethics" or "the morality of relativism." Applications of such concepts are very often in full-fledged rebellion against the older interpretation of the Ten Commandments, which insisted that they be understood as a stringently absolutist ethic. It is true, of course, that

Jesus himself, especially in his discourses on the meaning of Sabbath observance as well as in his commentary on the Decalogue as it is found in the Sermon on the Mount, taught that the Ten Commandments are subject to interpretation and that their full significance is not to be understood simply by quoting them verbatim. But Christ never went so far as to say that each individual, whether Christian or otherwise, possesses the moral and spiritual sensitivity to interpret them properly for himself. Always and in every situation we are to subject ourselves to the Bible, to the commandments of the Bible, and to the divinely given interpretations of the commandments as they are found in the Bible. By doing so we will demonstrate that we love God and that we are willing to admit that "his commands are not burdensome" (1 John 5:3). God, the sovereign Father of his chosen people, has laid down rules and regulations intended for our greatest good and his greatest glory. If we love him, we will do our utmost for his highest.

As our omnipotent and omniscient king, God exercises his sovereignty by determining for everyone "the times set for them and the exact places where they should live" (Acts 17:26). His decision concerning when and where all of us are to be born, to live, and to die is applicable to nations as well as to individuals. Pagan rulers are merely agents accomplishing his will (Isa. 44:24–45:3; Dan. 4). Those who trust in him can sing with the psalmist, "My times are in your hands" (Ps. 31:15). He has created us, he sustains us, and it is to him alone that we shall some day have to give account of our words and deeds.

As the beneficent owner of all that exists, God exercises his sovereignty by dispensing tokens of his bounty to whomever he will (Acts 17:24–25). At times we may be tempted to become envious of people who are more talented or attractive or wealthy than we are, or we may deplore the fact that we are merely average or less in so many areas. One way to conquer despondency at such times is to remember the old saying about the man who complained that he had no shoes until he met a man who had no feet. Another way is to remember to thank God frequently for the innumerable positive expressions of his goodness to us in supplying us with capacities and attributes that may seem unfair when compared with those of other people but that have proved again and again to be completely adequate to our own personal situations. Our response to God's giving to some while withholding from others should always be that of Christ: "Yes, Father, for this was your good pleasure" (Luke 10:21).

In his dealings with his children, God has displayed his sovereignty in numerous ways throughout history. The Old Testament constitutes a recital of his mighty acts in their behalf. We have already noted the demonstration of God's sovereign activity in creation, and it is thrilling indeed to observe the ways in which he has continued to relate himself to our world from that remote period to our own day. In the case of Abraham, for example, the sovereignty of God is everywhere apparent. Whenever Abraham attempted to assist God in accomplishing his purposes, total failure was the result. The Lord had told Abraham that he would make him into a great nation (Gen. 12:2), but Abraham's recognition of the barrenness of his wife Sarah caused him to doubt the validity of God's promise. He therefore embarked on a course of action that would guarantee that he would have a son to whom to pass on his estate.

In Old Testament times, adoption was one of the options available in such situations in the case of childless marriages. Archeological excavations were begun in 1925 at the ancient site of Nuzi, located near modern Kirkuk in Iraq. Hundreds of contract documents dating from the fifteenth century B.C. were uncovered during the course of the excavations. Although the patriarchs lived in Canaan a few centuries earlier than the fifteenth, the clay tablets from Nuzi throw a flood of light on the patriarchal period because customs ordinarily linger for many generations in the Middle East. We have learned from those tablets that it was legally permissible at Nuzi for a childless couple to adopt a son who would then become their heir. Often the man's chief slave would become the adopted son, a fact that helps us to understand Abraham's plea in Genesis 15:2–3: "O Sover-

eign LORD, what can you give me since I remain childless and
the one who will inherit my estate is Eliezer of Damascus? . . .
You have given me no children; so a servant in my household
will be my heir." Apparently Abraham had acquired Eliezer as a
servant when he had originally migrated from Ur of the
Chaldeans to Canaan. Subsequently, it would seem, Abraham
had adopted Eliezer in order that the slave, in his new capacity
as Abraham's son, might inherit his master's estate. As we have
seen, such a procedure was entirely legitimate in those days. In
response to Abraham's hasty action, however, the Lord said to
him, "This man will not be your heir, but a son coming from
your own body will be your heir" (15:4). The sovereignty of God
would overrule in Abraham's case, and Abraham's own firstborn,
the son of his wife, would exercise his legal claim over that of
the adopted son. God's perfect will would overwhelm Sarah's
barrenness, and Isaac would be born.

But Abraham either did not understand precisely what God
was going to do or his faith became impatient. We are told that,
at the instigation of Sarah, he cohabited with Hagar, Sarah's
Egyptian servant, in order to produce a son through her (16:1–4).
The Nuzi documents illustrate that such a practice was another
option in a household that had no male heir. If the lady of the
house failed to bear a son, one of the master's female servants
could be pressed into service to perform that function. If a son
was then born, in accordance with oriental custom he, instead
of an adopted slave, would become the heir, even though the
adoption had taken place earlier and in spite of the fact that the
newly born child was the son of a concubine. In the case of the
union of Abraham and Hagar, the result was Ishmael (16:15),
"born in the ordinary way" (Gal. 4:23). He, rather than Eliezer,
would now be heir to Abraham's property.

But once again God, in his sovereign wisdom, overruled. He
said to Abraham concerning Ishmael: "I will surely bless him;
I will make him fruitful and will greatly increase his numbers.
. . . But my covenant I will establish with Isaac, whom Sarah
will bear to you by this time next year" (Gen. 17:20–21). Nei-

ther Eliezer, the adopted servant, nor Ishmael, the son of a female servant, but Isaac, the son of Sarah "born by the power of the Spirit" (Gal. 4:29), "born as the result of a promise" (4:23), would receive the inheritance of Abraham and fulfill the will of God. As at Nuzi the rights of the firstborn son of the lady of the household eclipsed and superseded those of any other male children, whether adopted or servant-born, so also would the divinely ordained prerogatives of Isaac eliminate the privileges of Abraham's other sons and thereby further the plans and purposes of the sovereign God. This whole series of events may be viewed as yet another example of the fact that God's children are not permitted to do anything through their own strength or by means of their own resources to assist him in the fulfillment of his promises. An almighty God needs no help from his creatures.

Other scriptural illustrations of God's sovereignty throughout history are not hard to find. As Abraham failed miserably when he attempted to fulfill God's promises for him, so Moses was unable in his own strength to liberate his people from Egyptian bondage. The Lord displayed his limitless power in a series of astounding miracles that forced even the magicians of Pharaoh to exclaim, "This is the finger of God" (Exod. 8:19). The Lord hardened Pharaoh's heart in order to make all the more vivid the redemption of his people (7:3–5) and preserved the very life of Pharaoh in order to demonstrate his might and ensure that his name would be proclaimed throughout the earth (9:15–16). The keynote of the entire exodus experience is the awesome power and the absolute sovereignty of the one true God, celebrated in the Song of Moses and Miriam (15:1–18, 21).

The period of Israel's monarchy includes similar examples. Amos, the first of the writing prophets, typifies the conviction of his Old Testament colleagues in his vivid descriptions of the impartial manner in which God judges not only pagan nations (Amos 1:3–2:3) but also his own covenant people (2:4–16). He is always in complete control of human affairs: "When disaster comes to a city, has not the LORD caused it?" (3:6). Nowhere in the universe can one hide from him (9:2; Ps. 139:7–10), because he created the very stars of the heavens (Amos 5:8).

As God was sovereign in the individual and collective experience of people in ancient times, so is he sovereign in the world today. The failure of our generation to acknowledge his sovereignty does not mean it no longer exists. Sensitive Israelites of the Old Testament period watched with bated breath as individual sins and national conspiracies were in turn condemned and judged by God, and it is as true today as it ever was that "the One enthroned in heaven laughs; the Lord scoffs at them" (Ps. 2:4). If the concept of divine sovereignty makes today's unbeliever defiant or fearful, it causes the Christian to rejoice. We who belong to Christ know that the Father has delegated all authority to the Son, our Lord Jesus: "God placed all things under his feet and appointed him to be head over everything for the church, which is his body, the fullness of him who fills everything in every way" (Eph. 1:22–23).

3 Election

The Lord has chosen you.

Deuteronomy 14:2

One of the most prominent ways in which the one true God displayed his sovereignty throughout the Old Testament period was by exercising his indisputable right to make choices. Human beings share this right with God to a limited degree, but only the sovereign Lord of the universe experiences complete freedom as he chooses to embark upon or desist from a certain course of action. Divine choice is especially important to us as it relates to the purposes of God in predestining people as objects of his mercy and salvation. But he makes choices in other areas as well, and it is in the broadest possible sense that we should try to understand the biblical doctrine of election as one of the central themes of the Old Testament.

It is possible to detect God's elective purposes at least as far back as Genesis 10. That chapter, the so-called Table of Nations, is in fact a literary map of the entire ancient Near East. It describes the dispersion of the peoples of the then-known world after the flood "by their clans and languages, in their territories and nations" (Gen. 10:20, 31) in terms of the descendants of the sons of Noah, whose names were "Shem, Ham and Japheth" (10:1). The surrounding context (Gen. 9 and 11) makes it clear that God decided to concentrate on the family line of Shem as those who were to carry forward his plans of revelation and redemption. In these early chapters of the Bible, then, we first meet the Shemites or Semites, those nations who constituted the chosen people of God before the time of Abraham.

Unfortunately, people today are most familiar with the term *Semitic* in a negative sense. We hear much, for example, about anti-Semitic prejudice and the like. Something similar to such a deplorable attitude undoubtedly lies in the background of the question that is often raised about the suitability of Semitic peoples to be the objects of God's grace and love. Its crispest form may perhaps be found in this brief poem: "How odd / that God / should choose / the Jews!" Did God make a mistake in his election of the Semites? Are we to say that he was capricious and arbitrary in making his choice? Did he have cogent reasons for acting as he did? Would you and I have chosen differently?

All we can say for certain and without fear of contradiction is that the sovereign God always chooses the best peoples and individuals to carry out his purposes, even though we may not always be able to discern the reasons for his choices.

We next meet the elective purposes of God in the life of Abraham. After hurrying through the genealogies from Shem to Terah, the writer of Genesis tells us that God narrowed the scope of his election by concentrating on Abraham and his descendants. Out of all the Semitic peoples, God chose the family line of Abraham to carry out his will in the world. In recognition of the fact that Abraham is the first person in the Bible to be called a Hebrew (Gen. 14:13), his descendants have shared that designation with him.

Many have seen in God's call of Abraham from Ur of the Chaldeans and his divine election to blessing and prosperity an act of unfair partiality. Is not the God of the universe displaying a petty particularism by acting in such a way? If he is the God of the whole human race, how are we to explain such peculiar provincialism on his part? Is it proper for him to reserve all of his blessings for the descendants of a single individual?

The election of the Hebrew people, however, is not nearly so particularistic as it may seem at first glance. Even in God's great promises to Abraham as recorded in Genesis 12:3 and 22:18 is found the assurance that in him and his descendants *all* peoples and nations on earth would be blessed, an assurance later given to Isaac (26:4) and Jacob (28:14) as well. After the day of Pentecost Peter reminded his own countrymen of the ancient promise (Acts 3:25), and Paul applied it to Gentile Christians in his own day (Gal. 3:8). We can see, then, that the ultimately worldwide intention of God's election of Abraham is evident from the outset.

We should observe also that an important part of the divine promise to Abraham was the gracious gift of a homeland to his descendants. It is not merely coincidental that the land of Canaan, the crossroads of the ancient world, was chosen for that purpose. Located at the eastern end of the Mediterranean Sea, it was ideally situated to serve as a focal point for commercial, cultural, and religious interchange. It was God's plan for Canaan to serve as a staging area for the dissemination of vital and redemptive faith to the nations that surrounded the Hebrew people to whom he was to give the land. The reference of Ezekiel to Jerusalem's location "in the center of the nations, with countries all around her" (Ezek. 5:5), not only emphasizes the religious prominence of the Holy Land but also serves to remind us of the providential placement of God's people in the geographic sense as well.

Even among the pagan inhabitants of Canaan itself, there were those to whom God chose to reveal his redemptive love. Melchizedek was just such an individual. As the Canaanite priest of Jerusalem in the time of Abraham, Melchizedek was a worshiper of "God Most High" (Gen. 14:18–20), who, we now know, was the chief deity in the Canaanite pantheon. It would appear, however, that Abraham recognized in Melchizedek the makings of a true believer, because he identified Melchizedek's "God Most High" with "the LORD" (14:22). Two millennia later Paul, in a similar way, would begin at the level of religious knowledge of his Athenian hearers and would then proceed to reveal to them the true identity of their "unknown god" (Acts 17:23). Abraham, on his part, gives us an early demonstration of the same kind of missionary zeal and provides us with yet another illustration of the fact that God's election of the Hebrew people does not necessarily and automatically consign the rest of the human race to condemnation.

As we follow the thread of divine election subsequent to the time of Abraham, we arrive at a further narrowing down of God's purposes in his choice of Jacob and his descendants. In the story of Jacob's birth we have an excellent example of how God's sovereignty is interwoven with his elective decrees. We have already discussed in chapter 2 the importance of the firstborn son as the primary heir of the family estate. Deuteronomy 21:15–17 is a classic reference to the law of primogeniture, which meant that the firstborn son was to receive a "double share" of his father's inheritance. Therefore when Elisha said to Elijah, "Let me inherit a double portion of your spirit" (2 Kings 2:9), he was expressing his ardent desire to become, in reputation and in reality, the firstborn son of Elijah in a spiritual sense. We are probably to understand "double share" or "double portion" as referring to twice as much as that given to each of the remaining sons, regardless of how many there were. In any event the firstborn son, not a son born later on, received the lion's share of the estate.

It may come to us as a surprise at first to learn that the Lord said to Isaac's wife Rebekah, "Two nations are in your womb, and two peoples from within you will be separated; one people will be stronger than the other, and the older will serve the younger" (Gen. 25:23). In his sovereign elective plan, God was clearly overruling the ancient law of primogeniture in the case of these two male infants, Esau and Jacob. Jacob, and not the firstborn Esau, was ordained by God to receive the major portion of Isaac's inheritance. Upon reaching adulthood, Jacob, human to the core, cheated his brother out of his birthright as well as his blessing (27:36), but his despicable conduct did not cancel God's ultimate purposes for his life (Rom. 9:10–12). The

Lord still evaluated the two men and their descendants, relatively speaking, in these terms: "I have loved Jacob, but Esau I have hated" (Mal. 1:2–3). The significance of that divine evaluation was not lost on Paul, who made use of it as an illustration of individual election (Rom. 9:13–24).

Jacob's name was subsequently changed to Israel (Gen. 32:28; 35:10), and the Old Testament makes it abundantly clear that God's choice of Jacob extended to his descendants, the Israelites. Moses, speaking to the people of Israel beyond the Jordan in the desert, said to them, "The LORD your God has chosen you out of all the peoples on the face of the earth to be his people, his treasured possession" (Deut. 7:6). The context of this passage teaches us that "chosen" (7:6) and "set his affection on" (7:7) and "loved" (7:8) and "redeemed" (7:8) are related if not synonymous ideas. Election in such a biblical framework includes both love and redemption. If the question is asked, "What is the basis of God's election in this case? Why did he choose Israel?" the answer can only be given in the words of the text itself: "The LORD . . . set his affection on you . . . because the LORD loved you" (7:7–8). We should look for no more adequate a reason than that. God's grace is, indeed, amazing!

As we return to an investigation of Jacob's immediate family, we observe once again that God vetoed the law of primogeniture in his choice of Judah as the human instrument of his divine will. Reuben was Jacob's firstborn, while Judah occupied the fourth place in the chronologically arranged list of Jacob's sons (Gen. 29:32–35; 35:23). But it soon became evident that Judah possessed qualities of leadership that his brothers respected. When ten of Jacob's sons decided to rid themselves of their arrogant brother Joseph, Reuben and Judah both counseled moderation (37:21–27). But by the time Joseph, some years later, had been sold into slavery and had subsequently risen to prominence in Egypt, Judah had become the acknowledged spokesman of his brothers. He not only reported to his father the words of Joseph expressing the only conditions under which the brothers would be able to make a return trip to Egypt for supplies (43:1–10), but he also delivered an eloquent and crucial plea to Joseph, assuming the posture of a servant in doing so, just before Joseph revealed himself to his brothers (44:14–34). The rise of Judah to a position of supremacy among his brothers is also reflected in the action of Jacob who, we are told, "sent Judah ahead of him to Joseph to get directions to Goshen" (46:28). Thus the author of Genesis represents Judah, by no means Jacob's firstborn, as being under the special providential care of God.

The divine elective purposes extended to the descendants of Judah as well. As God had called out of the inhabited earth the Semitic nations, and as he had chosen from those nations the Hebrew people, and as he had selected from those people the sons of Israel, so also now the tribe of Judah would be the supreme object of his sovereign grace. One of the earliest among the Old Testament prophecies that are generally called messianic is that found in Genesis 49:10: "The scepter will not depart from Judah, nor the ruler's staff from between his feet, until he comes to whom it belongs and the obedience of the nations is his." Many have seen in this verse a veiled reference to the ultimate rule of Christ over the world. However that may be, at the very least it reflects the supremacy of the tribe of Judah. The Chronicler agrees with such an evaluation, because after listing the sons of Israel with Judah in the fourth position (1 Chron. 2:1) he then proceeds to set forth the names of the descendants of Judah in the next two and a half chapters (2:3–4:23). Only then is he prepared to tell us about the descendants of the other brothers, the tally of which is in every case briefer than that of Judah.

One of the main purposes of the Chronicler was to emphasize the positive aspects of the history of the tribe of Judah, particularly as they related to the story of David and his successors on the throne in Jerusalem. We have seen that the elective decrees of the sovereign God narrowed down progressively from the human race generally to the Semitic nations, and from there to the Hebrew people, and from there to the sons of Israel, and from there to the tribe of Judah. We are now prepared to observe the way in which God chose the family of David in another act of loving grace. The selection of David himself serves as yet another illustration of the divine revocation of the law of primogeniture (1 Sam. 16:1–13). The Lord told Samuel, whose privilege it was to anoint the first two rulers of united Israel, that the successor of Saul was to be found among the sons of Jesse. Beginning with the oldest, Jesse brought all but one of his sons to Samuel, "but Samuel said to him, 'The LORD has not chosen these'" (16:10). Jesse then called in his youngest son, David, from the fields where he had been pasturing his father's flocks. At the command of the Lord, "Samuel took the horn of oil and anointed him in the presence of his brothers, and from that day on the Spirit of the LORD came on David in power" (16:13).

Noteworthy in this connection is the statement made by the Lord to Samuel with respect to the process of choosing the second ruler of Israel. Although it applies to Jesse's sons specifically, it surely has implications for God's relationship to his children generally: "The LORD does not look at the things man looks at. Man looks at the outward appearance, but the LORD looks at the heart" (16:7).

The elective purposes of God may be discerned also with respect to the ancestry of David as well as to his posterity. One of the themes of the Book of Ruth is the glorious concept that the arms of God's love are not so short that they cannot enfold a Moabite maiden. To be sure, the Israelites were God's chosen people. But that fact did not deter the Lord from extending his grace to Ruth. Because of her willingness to accompany her mother-in-law Naomi from Moab to Bethlehem and to serve Naomi's God (Ruth 1:16), she became, in the course of time, the ancestress of King David (4:18–22). She remains to this day a choice example of the occasional transfusion of Gentile blood into the veins of the divinely chosen and essentially Israelite community.

With respect to David's posterity, Isaiah predicted that a shoot would come up from the stump of Jesse, a "Branch" would grow out of his roots, the Spirit of the Lord would rest upon him, and he would delight in the fear of the Lord (Isa. 11:1–3). No doubt

the people of Isaiah's time read this prophecy in terms of a powerful monarch of the Davidic line who would bring to them an
unparalleled period of peace and prosperity. In fact they were
convinced that, as God's chosen people and as the caretakers of
his temple (Jer. 7:4), they deserved such a king. They were prone
to forget that divine election and human responsibility are two
sides of the same coin. Amos 3:2 makes this concept very clear
as it records the word of the Lord to the northern kingdom of
Israel in the eighth century B.C.: "You only have I chosen of all
the families of the earth; therefore I will punish you for all your
sins." The people of God enjoy no privileged status, because
"from everyone who has been given much, much will be
demanded" (Luke 12:48). As the members of David's royal line
continued in their wicked ways down through the centuries, it
was inevitable that God would ultimately judge them. And so
he did. Zedekiah, the last of David's descendants on the throne
in Jerusalem, was forced to look on as Nebuchadnezzar's men
executed his sons, after which the eyes of Zedekiah himself were
put out (2 Kings 25:7).

In such a situation, who could possibly perform the function
of the "Branch"? The New Testament sees in "Jesus Christ the
son of David" (Matt. 1:1) the ultimate fulfillment of Isaiah's
prophecy. Matthew was probably thinking of Isaiah 11:1 when
he called Jesus a Nazarene in Matthew 2:23, because the Greek
word for *Nazarene* bears a striking resemblance to the Hebrew
word for *branch*. Paul said of David son of Jesse: "From this man's
descendants God has brought to Israel the Savior Jesus, as he
promised" (Acts 13:23). And in Romans 15:12 Paul quoted from
Isaiah 11:10 and applied it to Christ. It is therefore clear that
Jesus is represented in these and many other verses of the New
Testament as the one in whom are wrapped up all the messianic
prophecies of the Old Testament.

But the elective purposes of God did not cease with the coming of Christ. It is true, of course, that in one sense "no matter
how many promises God has made, they are 'Yes' in Christ"
(2 Cor. 1:20). But in an equally valid sense it is also true that we

as Christians share with the Savior, God's "Chosen One" (Luke 23:35), the title "God's elect" (Titus 1:1). The revelation of the Scriptures has often been compared with a tree whose root system resembles the divine elective decrees up to and including the patriarchal period, whose relatively restricted trunk corresponds to the outworking of God's will during the period from Moses to Christ, and whose leafy crown portrays the expansion of God's gracious purposes in the church since Pentecost. As believers of today we partake of the results of what has taken place before us in heaven and on earth.

We must never forget, however, that our election is totally unmerited and that in and of ourselves we are nothing. All that we are and have we owe to the gracious and aggressive love of God in Christ.

A student from Ethiopia was describing certain aspects of his national culture to his fellow students in an anthropology class at a Christian college in America. During the discussion period that followed, one of the students asked him if he was married. He replied in the negative and then added that he hoped to marry a young Ethiopian woman soon. When asked what she was like, he responded by saying that he did not know because his father was arranging the marriage. Aghast, an American student said, "But what if she's homely or something?"

The Ethiopian answered, "My father would never make a bad choice for me."

"Think of what you were when you were called. Not many of you were wise by human standards; not many were influential; not many were of noble birth. But God chose the foolish things of the world to shame the wise; God chose the weak things of the world to shame the strong. He chose the lowly things of this world and the despised things—and the things that are not—to nullify the things that are, so that no one may boast before him. It is because of him that you are in Christ Jesus, who has become for us wisdom from God—that is, our righteousness, holiness and redemption. Therefore, as it is written: 'Let him who boasts boast in the Lord' " (1 Cor. 1:26–31).

4 Covenant, I

I will establish my covenant with you.

Genesis 6:18

The decision that a man and a woman make to become husband and wife does not normally take place overnight. There is usually a period of courtship that may extend through several years. This is followed by a proposal on the part of the man. The woman may then request some time to think over the offer, and only when she agrees to marry the man has the decision become mutual and the engagement actual. But even then the union is not to be legally consummated until after the formal wedding ceremony has taken place and the entire process has been solemnized in writing. The all-important document in this procedure, complete with the signatures of bride, groom, and witnesses, is known as a marriage license.

Our modern world could hardly get along without such official contracts in many significant areas of its commercial and political life. Salesman and customer alike are well aware of the importance of reading the fine print before signing on the dotted line. The citizen figures and refigures his income and deductions before he submits his tax forms to the Internal Revenue Service. The art of diplomacy seeks to keep the gears of international relationships meshing smoothly by means of a never-ending stream of treaties and lesser compacts.

As it is today, so has it been since the earliest historical periods. Necessity is the mother of invention, we are told, and it is quite likely that the invention of writing came about because of the need to keep records of various kinds. Archeologists have uncovered a wealth of contractual material, including marriage compacts, commercial agreements, and peace treaties incised on clay and inked on papyrus and leather. To refer to formal documents of this kind the Old Testament uses the all-inclusive term *covenant.*

That the word *covenant* (or *treaty*) was employed in a secular sense in the Old Testament can easily be demonstrated: it appears in marital (Mal. 2:14), political (1 Kings 5:12), and other contexts. Far more frequently, however, *covenant* is found in its specifically redemptive and technical sense in the Bible. It refers to any formal agreement between God and man that possesses legal validity and that is eternally operative. The one true God who has revealed himself in the Scriptures and who is sovereign over all creation entered into various covenant relationships with his people as a striking means of furthering his own elective purposes. Many students of the Old Testament believe that the concept of covenant is the most fundamental and overarching theme in the entire Bible. However that may be, we may surely affirm that it is at least close to the heart of the Old Testament.

Archeological and literary research during the past sixty years have greatly enriched our knowledge of covenant ceremonies and of the structure of covenant documents in the ancient Near East. In 1933 a French expedition began to excavate the site of the old Amorite city of Mari, located near the west bank of the Euphrates River not far from the border of Iraq. Eventually the workers unearthed the town's royal archives, consisting of thousands of clay documents that vividly illustrate life in Mesopotamia during the eighteenth century B.C. The Nuzi letters, already mentioned in chapter 2, and the Mari tablets constitute our main extrabiblical written sources for information concerning the period of the patriarchs in Canaan. The Mari letters inform us of the practice of killing a donkey as a solemn means of confirming an oath of alliance between two peoples or nations. In much later times the Saracens would slaughter a camel for a similar purpose, while throughout the sweep of biblical history various animals were used in ceremonies of covenant solemnization (Gen. 15:9). A fine description of the basic details of such a ceremony is found in Jeremiah 34:18–20: "The men who have violated my covenant and have not fulfilled the terms of the covenant they made before me, I will treat like the calf they cut in two and then walked between its pieces. The leaders of Judah and Jerusalem, the court officials, the priests and all the people of the land who walked between the pieces of the calf, I will hand over to their enemies who seek their lives." The animal was killed and cut into two or more pieces. The parties to the covenant then aligned the pieces, if more than two, in two rows of equal length, after which they walked in dignified procession down the aisle formed by the pieces. It is quite likely also that they took an oath that may have sounded something like this: "If I violate the terms of this covenant, may my blood be spilled as the blood of this animal was spilled!" At any rate, it is clear that the shedding of blood was necessary for the confirmation of significant treaties in ancient times.

From an entirely different source we learn about the format of the ancient treaties themselves as they appeared during the time when the oldest sections of the Old Testament were being written. The two and a half centuries from about 1450 to about 1200 B.C. constitute the later and, in some respects, most glorious years of the existence of the Hittite Empire. The Hittites' loss of their iron monopoly toward the end of their existence as an imperial power coincided with and helped to bring about their defeat at the hands of the Sea Peoples, among whom were the Philistines. But during their heyday the Hittites signed both parity and suzerainty treaties with the nations on their borders.

We do not know whether the Hittites originated the covenant forms that characterize their international compacts. It may be simply an archeological accident that only Hittite examples of the forms we are about to discuss, particularly of the suzerainty type, have so far come to light. In any event, many of the Hittite covenants were made with the peoples and nations of Canaan, the land of the patriarchs and their descendants. This fact may help to explain the parallels we will be able to draw later on between the covenants of the Hittites and those of the Old Testament.

A parity treaty was the form taken by a covenant that was consummated between equals. For example, if the Hittite monarch concluded a treaty with his counterpart in Egypt, the two kings would confer on the terms of the agreement, make suggestions to each other, bargain back and forth, and so on. In every respect the relationship between the two nations would be one of parity in such a situation.

But if the Hittites had just conquered one of the many smaller nations of the Near East on the field of battle, a suzerainty treaty, imposed by the Hittite king, would be in order. In a situation of this kind the vassal ruler and his subjects would have nothing to say about the stipulations of the covenant but would be compelled to submit to the demands of the Hittite suzerain. It is instructive to note in detail the formal literary structure of the typical suzerainty covenant of this period.

The first statement, which may be called the preamble, serves to identify the suzerain himself. It does so in grandiose terms: "Thus says So-and-so, the great king, the king of the land of the Hittites, the son of So-and-so, . . . the valiant one." Following this introduction is normally a historical prologue that outlines in detail the relationships that have obtained between the suzerain and the vassal up to the time of the treaty. The suzerain would naturally be careful to mention all of his benevolent actions on behalf of the vassal and all of the vassal's rebellious responses toward him. The third major item consists of the main body of the covenant document, the stipulations themselves. The relentless logic of the ever-present order of preamble—prologue—stipulations runs something like this: On the basis of the first section, which states who the suzerain is, and on the basis of the second section, which indicates what the suzerain has done for the vassal in the past, the third section states in explicit detail the duties and obligations of the vassal as imposed upon him by the suzerain. The stipulations warn the vassal not to enter into entangling alliances with other powers or to embark upon hostile ventures against the suzerain or his allies.

In addition to these three main sections, which by their very nature characterize all such suzerainty covenants, three other items are also frequently (but not always) found in them, although not necessarily in the following order. One of them is a paragraph regarding the blessings that will come if the vassal obeys the suzerain and the curses that will follow if he disobeys. A second is a statement that provides for the deposit of the covenant in a safe place and for the public reading of the terms of the covenant at periodic intervals. The third and final item is a list of witnesses to the document consisting of the names of the gods and goddesses of both the suzerain and his vassal.

By virtue of such extrabiblical parallels as we have already noted above, our understanding of the theological concept of covenant in the Old Testament has increased immeasurably with respect to its basic meaning and literary framework as well as to its ceremonial accompaniments. It goes without saying that covenant relationships between God and man as expressed in the Bible are never established on a basis of parity. God and his creatures do not come to the conference table as equals. They do not share in the formulation of the covenant stipulations. God does not ask us for our opinions regarding items to be included or excluded. The Lord of the universe does not abdicate his position of sovereignty when he enters into solemn agreements with his people. All such divine-human encounters in the Bible are referred to in terms of suzerainty rather than parity. Just as the vassal had no right to make suggestions to the Hittite king when the latter was drawing up a treaty that would affect them both, so also God does not consult his people when he binds them to himself, and himself to them, in earnest and permanent association.

This is not to say that biblical covenants are entirely one-sided or that God is the only active partner in his agreements with his people. God, who is perfectly righteous, sets the conditions of his covenants and brings to them his holiness, his justice, his grace and love. But God's people also have a part to play in the total relationship. They are requested to respond with faith and obedience and love. Biblical covenants may be properly described as unilateral, then, only to the extent that they are formulated by God and by him alone.

As we now begin our survey of the major redemptive covenants of the Old Testament period, we shall frequently refer to the light shed on them by the developments in Near Eastern research already mentioned in this chapter. We shall observe that in every case a knowledge of ancient covenant practices will be of assistance to us in the interpretation of one or more details.

The story of the Lord's covenant with Noah is recorded in Genesis 9:8–17. That it is a covenant of suzerainty is clear from God's opening statement: "I now establish my covenant with you and with your descendants after you" (9:9). The fact that the Lord agrees never again to destroy all living things by means of a flood without at the same time requiring a response of some sort on Noah's part makes the Noahic covenant rather unusual. Its nature is clearly represented as being unconditional from the outset. It is also described as "everlasting" (9:16), and we are thereby reminded that covenants in ancient times were typically stated to remain effective "for all future time." After investigating this matter with respect to about 7,500 "eternal" treaties signed between about 1500 B.C. and about A.D. 1850, a historian reported that the treaties in question lasted an average of only two years each! Needless to say, our God will never revoke the everlasting covenants that he made with Noah or with any other Old Testament believer. This does not mean, however, that such covenants cannot be broken from the side of God's people when there is opportunity for them to do so (Isa. 24:5; Jer. 31:32).

The Lord often gave his people a sign when he established a covenant with them. Such signs were to serve as reminders to them of his gracious provisions for their welfare. In the case of the Noahic covenant the sign was the "rainbow in the clouds" (Gen. 9:13). From that time forward the rainbow would become, for all who had eyes to see, a token of God's solemn promise never again to overwhelm all of his creatures with devastating flood waters. God had spoken, and he would bring his word to remembrance every time the rain fell.

Genesis 15 and 17 share the account of the Lord's covenant with Abraham. In particular, Genesis 15:7–21 is a passage that illustrates several aspects of ancient Near Eastern covenant structure and solemnization. As the Hittite monarch identified himself in the preambles of his covenants, so also does the God of Abraham reveal himself to his vassal: "I am the LORD" (15:7). As the king of the Hittites then recounted the past history of his relationships with the subject ruler, so does God give a brief résumé of his dealings with Abraham up to this point: "I . . . brought you out of Ur of the Chaldeans to give you this land to take possession of it" (15:7). And as the "great king" continued by listing the terms of the covenant so that his vassal would know what was expected of him, so also does the Great King share with Abraham, in two installments (15:13–16, 18–21), his plans for Abraham, his descendants, and the land of Canaan. Thus the three main features of the Hittite suzerainty treaty are all found in the description of the structure of the Abrahamic covenant in Genesis 15.

More important for a proper understanding of covenant practices in ancient times, however, is the portrayal in Genesis 15 of the way in which such covenants were solemnized. The Lord commanded Abraham to gather several animals including a heifer, a goat, a ram, and two birds (15:9). Having collected the animals, Abraham slaughtered them and then bisected them. He did not cut the birds in two, however, probably because of their small size (15:10–11). Because of the custom of cutting animals in two in connection with the covenant-making ceremony, the Old Testament uses the technical expression "cut a covenant" in the sense of "make a covenant." For example, Genesis 15:18 describes the situation idiomatically when it states: "On that day the LORD made a covenant" with Abraham. A more literal translation of the Hebrew original would read as follows: "On that day the LORD *cut* a covenant."

After bisecting the animal carcasses Abraham laid the several halves in two rows of equal length to form an aisle (as described earlier in this chapter). Under ordinary circumstances, it would then have been appropriate for the two parties to the covenant to march in single file and in solemn procession down the aisle. By so doing they would have indicated their intention to abide by the covenant stipulations and to follow them to the letter. But in the story before us we are told only that "a smoking firepot with a blazing torch . . . passed between the pieces" (15:17). Needless to say, we are to understand these fiery objects as referring to theophanies (appearances of God in visible form). The Lord was often seen by his people in the midst of fires of various kinds. To Moses, God (in the form of the angel of the Lord) appeared "in flames of fire from within a bush" that, though burning, "did not burn up" (Exod. 3:2–4). Many years later Moses brought the people of Israel out of the desert camp to meet God at the holy mountain, "and Mount Sinai was covered with smoke, because the LORD descended on it in fire" (19:18). Through a period of forty years in "that vast and dreadful desert" (Deut. 1:19), "by day the LORD went ahead of them in a pillar of cloud to guide them on their way and by night in a pillar of fire to give them light" (Exod. 13:21). In the contest on Mount Carmel between the Lord and Baal during the early years of the divided monarchy, Elijah demonstrated the clarity of his theological perception by observing that "the god who answers by fire—he is God" (1 Kings 18:24). Having soaked his altar and sacrifice with water, Elijah stood back and watched quietly as "the fire of the LORD fell and burned up the sacrifice, the wood, the stones and the soil, and also licked up the water in the trench" (18:38). Although the reference to the "tongues of fire" (Acts 2:3) that accompanied the coming of the Holy Spirit on the day

of Pentecost may well be figurative, the background of the statement is clearly to be sought in those Old Testament passages
that describe fiery theophanies. And the biblical appearances of
God in fiery forms and shapes began with the smoking firepot
and blazing torch of Genesis 15:17. God committed himself to
his covenant with Abraham by passing between the pieces of the
slaughtered animals.

But was not Abraham himself also a party to the covenant?
Why did he not march down the aisle as well? The record emphasizes the fact that the Abrahamic covenant was a suzerainty agreement by stressing the passive characteristics of Abraham's par-
ticipation. The details are not completely clear, but it would
seem that after Abraham prepared the animals he fell into a deep
sleep and remained in that condition throughout the rest of the
ritual of solemnization (15:12). This fact, coupled with the real-
ization that no mention is made of Abraham's walking between
the rows of animal pieces, demonstrates that God was estab-
lishing a unilateral compact with his servant.

Genesis 17 describes another phase of the Abrahamic covenant
and contributes further toward a fuller understanding of it. In
the preamble the Lord again identifies himself to Abraham, this
time by saying, "I am God Almighty" (17:1). In this case there
is no historical recapitulation of past relationships between the
suzerain and his vassal, perhaps because nothing significant had
happened since the events recorded in Genesis 15. At any rate,
a number of details are added to the stipulations of the previous
covenant statement. They deal mainly with God's promise to
make Abraham "the father of many nations" (17:4), a promise
underscored by the change of his name from Abram ("Exalted
Father") to Abraham ("Father of Many," 17:5). In the course of
time God would also announce to Isaac that the descendants of
Abraham, and therefore of Isaac as well, would be exceedingly
numerous (17:19; 26:4).

While no conditions were attached to the divinely ordained
Noahic covenant, the Abrahamic covenant is represented as being
conditional. God had every right to demand of Abraham and his

descendants obedience with respect to the covenant stipulations (17:9–10). It is also clear that although the Abrahamic covenant was everlasting from God's standpoint (17:7, 13, 19), it could be broken by disobedient human participants (17:14). God's test of Abraham in Genesis 22 loses its force unless we assume that he could have chosen to disobey the Lord if he had so desired. In fact, the Lord renewed his promise of blessing to Abraham and his descendants on the basis of Abraham's faithfulness to the Lord's demands (22:18). To Isaac also God confirmed his previous announcement of numerous progeny "because Abraham obeyed me and kept my requirements, my commands, my decrees and my laws" (26:5).

As the sign of the Noahic covenant was the rainbow, the sign of the Abrahamic covenant was circumcision (17:11). From that time forward the rite of circumcision would become, for every Israelite who had eyes to see, a token of God's solemn promise to bless his people numerically. God had spoken, and he would bring his word to remembrance every time the circumciser's knife was wielded. As observers of this most significant ritual, perceptive Israelites would be reminded that God's covenants are always sealed with blood.

5

Covenant, 2

Obey me fully and keep my covenant.
Exodus 19:5

Of the many agreements between God and his people described in the Old Testament, none is so significant or has such far-reaching implications as the Sinaitic or Mosaic covenant. The word *testament* as used in the King James Version of the Bible is almost always a synonym for *covenant*. In fact, we would be more correct in referring to the two major divisions of our Bibles as the Old and New Covenants than as the Old and New Testaments. The phrase *New Covenant*, or *New Testament*, is most precisely applied to the redemptive agreement that was consummated between God and the human race on Mount Golgotha in the first century, an agreement that was sealed with the blood of our Lord. The story of that covenant lies at the heart of the New Testament. The phrase *Old Covenant*, or *Old Testament*, is most accurately applied to the redemptive agreement that was consummated between God and the Israelite nation on Mount Sinai, an agreement that was sealed with the blood of sacrificial animals. The story of that covenant lies at the heart of the Old Testament.

The desert setting for the establishment of the Mosaic covenant is described in Exodus 19–24, and these chapters are there-

fore crucial for a proper understanding of the details of the transaction. The record informs us that the Sinaitic covenant, like
the Abrahamic covenant, was conditional. Exodus 19:5 makes
it clear that God's covenant blessings would be contingent upon
the willingness of the Israelites to abide by its stipulations: "Now
if you obey me fully and keep my covenant, then out of all
nations you will be my treasured possession." Three times, we
are told, the people agreed to be obedient (19:8; 24:3, 7). Subsequent history would outline the many occasions on which
Israel would backslide from its original glad response to God's
overtures, but at least at the beginning they expressed their intention to follow the Lord's leading through his servants.

Exodus 24 seems to allude to the traditional ritual of solemnization that accompanied the covenant-making procedure and
that has already been discussed in detail in chapter 4. The slaughter of animals appears again as an important part of the entire
process (24:5). This time, however, the parties to the covenant
do not walk down an aisle formed by sections of slaughtered animals. Instead we find Moses sprinkling half of the blood of the
animals against the sacrificial altar (24:6) and half on the people
themselves (24:8). We are probably to understand these strange
actions as constituting an alternate way of symbolizing the willingness of the participants to abide by the terms of the covenant.
The altar here represents the Lord's side of the agreement, and
the people's submission to the ritual action represents their side.
Moses' manipulation of "the blood of the covenant" (24:8) thus
takes on significance as the visible means of drawing together
God and his people.

We have already become familiar with the literary structure
of the ancient Hittite treaties and have observed how the various elements of that structure reappear in the covenants of the
Old Testament. Exodus 19:4–6 exhibits the three basic elements
of the covenant outline in brief form. The first of the three, the
self-identification of the suzerain in the preamble, is implicit in
the use of the word "I" twice in 19:4. The second, the historical prologue, is beautifully expressed in the same verse: "You

yourselves have seen what I did to Egypt, and how I carried you on eagles' wings and brought you to myself." The stipulations themselves, which constitute the third element, are summarized in a general way in 19:5–6. A new point of contact between biblical covenants and the Hittite treaties that form their literary background is the use here of the term *words* (19:6) in the technical sense of "covenant stipulations."

Many people are surprised to learn that the familiar title usually given to Exodus 20:2–17 and Deuteronomy 5:6–21, the Ten Commandments, should be rendered more literally wherever it appears (Exod. 34:28; Deut. 4:13; 10:4) as "the ten words." The word *Decalogue* (from Greek *deka*, "ten," and *logos*, "word"), another name often applied to the Ten Commandments, expresses the idea exactly. Exodus 20:1 introduces the Ten Commandments in this way: "God spoke all these words." And *words*, in Hittite treaties and in covenant contexts of the type before us, means specifically "covenant stipulations." It is used in this way in the Hebrew text of Exodus 19:6–7 and 24:3, 4, 8. All of these considerations make it evident that the Ten Commandments are a capsule condensation of the Sinaitic covenant.

The Decalogue begins with the familiar preamble, here expressed in its most solemn form: "I am the LORD your God" (Exod. 20:2). The historical prologue that follows, abbreviated in length, is majestic in its simplicity: "I . . . brought you out of Egypt, out of the land of slavery." The covenant stipulations, the "words," the commandments themselves, next make their appearance. It is as if the Lord were saying to his people, "Because of who I am, and because of what I have done for you, here is what you are required to do from this day forward: You shall have no other gods before me. . . ." The repetition of the Decalogue in Deuteronomy 5:6–21 also places it in a clearly covenantal context. The account is preceded by the use of the word *covenant* twice (5:2, 3), and the stipulations are referred to by the technical term *words* in the Hebrew text of 5:22. That verse adds another familiar piece of information by reminding us that the Lord wrote the Ten Commandments "on two stone tablets."

It is quite common to divide the Ten Commandments into two unequal groups, one a series of four religious commandments and the other a series of six moral or ethical injunctions. The statement of Jesus in Matthew 22:37–40 gives a considerable degree of credence to such a division, and there is nothing inherently wrong with it. There is no evidence, however, that would give us the right to assume that the division of the Ten Commandments in such a way is also confirmed by the statement that they were written "on two stone tablets," as though the first four were inscribed on the first tablet and the last six on the second. Such an assertion reads more into the text than is there. How, then, are we to understand the Old Testament references to "two stone tablets" (Exod. 31:18; 34:1; Deut. 4:13; 5:22; 10:1)? Once again, help has come to us unexpectedly from our knowledge of Hittite custom. Two copies of every Hittite suzerainty treaty were always made, one for the suzerain and one for the vassal. Needless to say, each copy contained the text of the entire treaty. So also it is plausible to assume that each of the two stone tablets described in the Bible contained the text of the entire Decalogue. One of the copies belonged to God and the other to God's covenant people, but both were stored in the ark of the covenant.

The preservation of ancient covenants in safe places not only emphasized the official and legal nature of such agreements but also ensured that they would always be available for consultation. Since the provisions of suzerainty treaties were applicable in perpetuity, it was necessary to remove them from their vaults from time to time for the purpose of proclaiming their contents publicly. In such a way the vassal and his subjects would be continually reminded of their duties and obligations toward their suzerain. Often the public reading would assume the form of a solemn covenant-renewal ceremony. We thus find Moses saying to the people of Israel in Deuteronomy 5:1–3: "Hear, O Israel, the decrees and laws I declare in your hearing today. Learn them and be sure to follow them. The LORD our God made a covenant with us at Horeb. It was not with our fathers that the LORD made this covenant, but with us, with all of us who are alive here today."

We must exercise caution in our attempts to understand this passage. Although Moses here seems to be denying the original divine establishment of the Sinaitic covenant with the previous generation of Israelites (5:3), he obviously cannot be doing so since he himself had been there at the time as the chief witness to the transaction. Moses is simply emphasizing the fact that a treaty concluded in a former generation is of no effect unless the present generation is also willing to abide by its stipulations. He therefore calls upon the new generation to pledge anew its loyalty to God. The same idea is expressed in a slightly different way in Deuteronomy 29:1: "These are the terms [literally, 'words'] of the covenant the LORD commanded Moses to make with the Israelites in Moab, in addition to the covenant he had made with them at Horeb." It has indeed become increasingly evident in recent years that the entire Book of Deuteronomy is neither more nor less than a lengthy covenant-renewal document with respect to literary form and that the verse just cited applies primarily to the main body of the book, the section comprising the stipulations, referred to here by the technical term *words*. Underscoring this point is the fact that the Hebrew title of Deuteronomy is "These Are the Words" or, more simply, "Words."

When we examine in detail the outline of Deuteronomy, we observe that it contains a section corresponding to each of the six main elements found in representative Hittite treaties of the period from about 1450 to about 1200 B.C. As we noted in chapter 4, these elements consist of a preamble, a historical prologue, a series of stipulations, a statement providing for the deposit and periodic public reading of the document, a list of witnesses, and a section that promises blessings and threatens curses depending on the reader's treatment of the terms of the covenant.

The first six verses of Deuteronomy identify the suzerain (God) and his deputy (Moses) and remind the Israelites assembled in the land of Moab that forty years had elapsed since God had revealed himself to them at Horeb. The historical prologue, which continues through to the end of Deuteronomy 4, recapitulates the events of the desert wanderings and reviews the ways in which the Lord had guided and provided for his people as well as the occasions on which they had rebelled against him. The prologue also forms the basis for the third main section of Deuteronomy, the stipulations themselves (5:1–27:10), beginning with the covenant summary embodied in the Ten Commandments and continuing in hortatory fashion with the promulgation of numerous laws, decrees, and requirements. These three main elements of covenant literary structure, as we have already seen, are characteristic of most formal biblical and extrabiblical agreements that have come down to us from ancient times and are always found in the same order.

The Book of Deuteronomy, as an expanded renewal of the Mosaic covenant, also contains the other three elements that tended to appear less frequently and in various orders in other contemporary treaty documents. The first such item is the blessings and curses formulae that constitute the main emphasis of 27:11–30:20. The curses were to be pronounced from Mount Ebal and the blessings from Mount Gerizim (11:29; 27:12, 13), both in the region of Shechem. Mount Gerizim became not only a symbol of blessing but also the site of a sanctuary built centuries later by the Samaritans. It was toward that mountain that a woman of Samaria pointed later still when she said to Jesus, "Our fathers worshiped on this mountain" (John 4:20). To this day, it is considered to be a sacred mountain by the few remaining survivors of the Samaritans.

Next, Deuteronomy 31:1–29 is concerned with providing for the safe deposit and periodic public reading of the covenant here being renewed. The section also stipulates the way in which an orderly continuity of leadership would be ensured for Israel after Moses' death. The covenant documents themselves were to be protected in close association with the ark of the covenant (31:26). They were to be read aloud to the people of Israel assembled in holy convocation once every seven years (31:10–13) as frequent reminders of the responsibilities to which the tribes had voluntarily committed themselves. Shortly before the death of Moses, the Lord commissioned Joshua to be his successor (31:23;

see also 34:9). The section concludes with the Song of Moses
(32:1–43) and the Blessing of Moses (33:2–29), the last legacy
of the great lawgiver to his beloved people.

The final element to be noted in the renewal covenant embodied in Deuteronomy is the list of witnesses attesting to its legal-
ity. As we observed in chapter 4, such a list in the typical Hittite suzerainty treaty would consist of the names of the gods and
goddesses of the king and his vassal. The witnesses to the
covenant stipulations in Deuteronomy are heaven and earth
(30:19; 31:28), which Moses invokes at the beginning of his
above-mentioned song (32:1).

After the conquest of most of Canaan, Moses' successor Joshua
gathered all the tribes of Israel together at Shechem for the first
covenant-renewal ceremony to take place in the promised land
itself (Josh. 24:1, 25). The proceedings emphasize the requirement of obedience on the part of the people (24:16–18, 21, 24),
once again stressing the conditional nature of the Sinaitic
covenant. We observe also that all six sections of the ancient
covenant literary structure are present in this one brief chapter.
First, Joshua identifies the suzerain as "the LORD, the God of
Israel" (24:2). Next appears the historical prologue, in this case
the longest section in the document (24:2–13). It traces God's
gracious activity in the lives of his people from the migrations
of Abraham to the military campaigns of Joshua himself. The
third item, the section containing the stipulations, is quite brief
and consists of two parts (24:14–15 and 24:23), each of which
demands total allegiance to the one true God and complete
refusal to worship other so-called gods. Provision for the preservation and remembrance of the covenant, the fourth element in
the structure, is likewise brief: "Joshua recorded these things in
the Book of the Law of God. Then he took a large stone and set
it up there under the oak near the holy place of the LORD"
(24:26). The fifth item, the curses and blessings formulae,
appears in a condensed summary in 24:20. The final section is
divided into two parts and represents the witnesses to the terms
of the covenant as being both the people themselves (24:22) and

the stone (24:27) mentioned earlier. It can thus be seen that
Joshua was concerned to follow the patterns sanctioned by long
usage in the culture of his time and blessed by the God of his
illustrious predecessor Moses.

We have no way of knowing how often the Mosaic covenant
was renewed in public ceremony in subsequent generations. The
Old Testament, selective in scope and journalistic in style, does
not pretend to give us every detail of Israel's history. In 2 Kings
22:3–23:25, however, mention is made of such a covenant-
renewal ceremony, perhaps because it was quite likely the last
example of its kind before the destruction of Jerusalem and the
exile of Judah in 586 B.C. King Josiah, we are told, "renewed the
covenant in the presence of the LORD—to follow the LORD and
keep his commands, regulations and decrees with all his heart
and all his soul, thus confirming the words of the covenant written in this book. Then all the people pledged themselves to the
covenant" (2 Kings 23:3). The occasion for this solemn ceremony was the discovery of an ancient book during the process
of cleaning and repairing the temple of Solomon after years of
neglect and disuse. The volume in question is called "the Book
of the Law" (22:8) and "the words of the covenant" (23:3),
phrases that are both used of Deuteronomy itself (Deut. 31:26;
29:9). It is also called "the Book of the Covenant" (2 Kings 23:2),
a title given to the expanded commentary on the Decalogue
found in Exodus 20:22–23:33 (Exod. 24:7). Josiah's long-lost
lawbook may therefore have been basically the Book of
Deuteronomy together with some additional Mosaic materials.
Whatever its contents, it was sufficient to evoke mourning and
repentance on the part of King Josiah, who "tore his robes"
(2 Kings 22:11) when it was read to him.

The prophets of Israel from the time of Amos and onward
were not unaware of the covenant relationship that should have
formed the normal bond of union between the Lord and his
people. Hosea (4:1–2) and Micah (6:2–6) stressed the legal
nature of the relationship, indicating that the Lord had a perfect right to sue Israel in a court of law for breach of contract.

But they and their fellow prophets used a number of other word pictures as well to portray as vividly as possible God's covenant love and steadfast loyalty. In elective grace, God had "chosen" his people (Isa. 49:7). As an expectant gardener, God had "planted" his vineyard (5:1–7). Like a doting father, God had "trained" and "called" his son (Hos. 7:15; 11:1). Most strikingly of all, as a devoted husband God had said to Israel, "I gave you my solemn oath and entered into a covenant with you, . . . and you became mine" (Ezek. 16:8).

Hosea developed to the fullest extent the imagery of the marriage between the Lord and Israel. As the verb *to know* is often used in the Bible for the most intimate relationship that can exist between a man and his wife (see the Hebrew text of Gen. 4:1 and the Greek text of Matt. 1:25), so also did the Lord say to Israel: "I cared for [literally, 'knew'] you in the desert" (Hos. 13:5). It is clear, then, that God himself initiated the relationship and that he did so at a specific time in history: "I am the Lord your God, who brought you out of Egypt" (12:9; 13:4). The Lord wooed his people to himself during the redemptive experience connected with the exodus and sealed the resulting marriage by means of the Sinaitic covenant. Israel, however, proved herself unfaithful by breaking the covenant (8:1) and committing spiritual adultery (2:2–13). Then God once again provided a remarkable display of his amazing grace by promising to win back Israel's love: "I will betroth you to me forever; I will betroth you in righteousness and justice, in love and compassion. I will betroth you in faithfulness, and you will acknowledge the Lord" (2:19–20). The love of God would not be denied, for he could not give up his chosen bride (11:8–9).

The teaching of Hosea concerning God's covenant love prepared the way for Jeremiah's doctrine of the "new covenant" (Jer. 31:31–34). Josiah, the last of Judah's reforming kings, had died on the battlefield at Megiddo in 609 b.c. Since that year a succession of wicked rulers had occupied the throne in Jerusalem, and it was evident to Jeremiah that the nation had passed the point of no return and was ripe for judgment. Shortly before the final, divinely appointed blow descended on Judah in 586, Jeremiah prophesied that the day would come, at an unspecified future time, when the Lord would make a new covenant to replace the old. In many respects the new agreement would not be like the one that his unfaithful "wife" of so many years had broken over and over again. Unlike the old covenant, inscribed on tablets of stone, the new covenant would be written on the hearts of God's people. The old covenant formula—"I will be their God, and they will be my people" (31:33; see also Ezek. 37:26–27)—would take on new meaning, because intimate knowledge of the Lord accompanied by the forgiveness of sins would become commonplace (Jer. 31:34).

Although Jeremiah himself may not have known the full significance of what he was saying, such a desirable state of affairs in the history of God's dealings with his people did take place several centuries later. The first communion meal shared by Jesus and his disciples inaugurated a new series of covenant-renewal ceremonies as proclaimed in Christ's own words of institution: "This cup is the new covenant in my blood; do this, whenever you drink it, in remembrance of me" (1 Cor. 11:25). Our Lord thus became "the mediator of a new covenant, that those who are called may receive the promised eternal inheritance—now that he has died as a ransom to set them free from the sins committed under the first covenant" (Heb. 9:15). The author of the letter to the Hebrews continues the passage by reminding us that the covenant in which Jesus participated, which he describes in terms of a last will and testament, could not be effective until the testator had died. The new covenant was thereby sealed with the blood of the Savior. How lavish is the love of God, and how extravagant was the price paid for our redemption!

6  Theocracy

The LORD reigns, let the earth be glad.

Psalm 97:1

During the latter half of the first century, at the very time when the early Christians were engaged in writing many of the books of the New Testament, Flavius Josephus, the greatest Jewish historian of his day, was producing an important series of volumes that describe in detail many aspects of the life of his people from the earliest times down to his own. In the second book of his polemic against the Egyptian writer Apion, Josephus portrays Moses' establishment of a system of government for the Israelite nation in these terms (according to the classic translation by Henry St. John Thackeray): "Some peoples have entrusted the supreme political power to monarchies, others to oligarchies, yet others to the masses. Our lawgiver, however, was attracted by none of these forms of polity, but gave to his constitution the form of what—if a forced expression be permitted—may be termed a 'theocracy,' placing all sovereignty and authority in the hands of God. To Him he persuaded all to look, as the author of all blessings, both those which are common to all mankind, and those which they had won for themselves by prayer in the crises of their history" (*Against Apion* 2.164–66).

This passage from the works of Josephus seems to indicate that he himself coined the word *theocracy.* At any rate, it has become the most common term used to designate the form of government that arose in Israel on the basis of the Sinaitic covenant during the period of the judges. In its strictest sense a theocracy would be a government under the immediate authority of God apart from the agency of human representatives. Israel rarely, if ever, experienced theocracy in so pure a form. More broadly conceived, however, the term applies to any political system in which God is believed to rule through his priests, ministers, or other deputies. In this expanded sense the monarchies from Saul through Zedekiah and the basically hierocratic government of Judah after the exile may be described as theocratic in form. It is also in this sense that theocracy lies close to the heart of the Old Testament.

Far from dying out with the destruction of Jerusalem in A.D. 70, a destruction witnessed by Josephus himself, the theocratic concept has continued to be employed by various nations, cultures, and religious groups down to the present time. In its early years Islam was theocratic in both principle and practice as the sword of Allah systematically cut down Muhammad's enemies, whether political or spiritual. During the High Middle Ages, some claimed that the papacy was a theocracy. Modern Roman Catholicism maintains only a few scattered traces of its former temporal glory, such as the title of the pope as the "Vicar of Christ" and the occupancy of Vatican City, an autonomous municipality in the heart of Rome. The Massachusetts Puritans of the early colonial period believed that God rules explicitly in the affairs of humankind, and they conducted their political life accordingly. The phrase "divine right of kings" summarizes much of the theocratic thinking that took place in Europe in the centuries immediately following the Protestant Reformation. It is the doctrine that hereditary monarchy is divinely ordained and that oppressed or otherwise unhappy citizens have no other recourse than to submit unquestioningly to the royal authority. The Stuart rulers of England and Scotland and Louis XIV of France were among its most prominent exponents. Although the American democratic system is in many respects a reaction against such ideas, certain sects on the fringe of American Protestantism, among them the Mormons and Jehovah's Witnesses, make use of theocratic elements either in their ecclesiastical organization or in their eschatological exposition.

Needless to say, the idea that the deity is supreme in power and authority in the political as well as the spiritual realm was held generally by ancient peoples and specifically by Semites. The consonantal group *m-l-k* was used by Semites of the Old Testament period to form numerous words that have to do with ruling or kingship. Many of these words are contained within proper names found in Scripture and may be detected by simply looking for the above-mentioned consonantal sequence or its equivalent. That the Semite frequently referred to his deity as "king" may be demonstrated, for example, by noting that the god of the Ammonites is called variously "Molech" (1 Kings 11:7) or "Milcom" (11:5, 33). With infinitely superior justification the people of Israel called the one true God "the King" (Ps. 95:3; 98:6; Isa. 6:5; Jer. 51:57) and spoke often of the fact that "the LORD reigns" (Ps. 96:10; 97:1; 99:1) as a testimony to their belief in his sovereignty over them. They also often gave their children names that had a distinctly theocratic flavor, such as Malkijah (1 Chron. 6:40), which means "The Lord Is My King"; Malkiel (7:31), meaning "God Is My King"; and Elimelech (Ruth 1:2), which may be translated "My God Is King."

From these few examples it can be seen that the concept of divine rule over people's lives was common in ancient times. Since the nations surrounding Israel placed their trust not in the one true God but in other so-called gods, theocracy for them remained in the realm of faith and was never translated into reality. As we attempted to demonstrate in chapter 1, God is one. He brooks no rivals, whether real or imaginary. As a part of his gracious elective program, however, God established with Israel a covenant that included a corpus of legislation intended to assist them in maintaining proper relationships with him and with each other. The highly organized system that arose out of the Sinaitic covenant was not only moral and ethical but also political in its thrust. We now turn to the story of the origin and development of Israel's theocracy.

Deuteronomy is the single most informative book in the Old Testament for a proper understanding of Israelite theocratic origins, although the other Mosaic documents make their contribution as well. At Mount Sinai the Lord "was king over Jeshurun when the leaders of the people assembled, along with the tribes of Israel" (Deut. 33:5). This passage from the blessing of Moses, in which Israel is called by her poetic name Jeshurun, is paralleled by the more straightforward account in Exodus 19, parts of which we discussed in chapter 5 in connection with the Sinaitic covenant. The careful distinction often made in our day between church and state would have been meaningless to Old Testament worshipers. For them, religious and civil matters were inseparable. Life for the Israelite people was so much a unity that they were utterly unable to compartmentalize it into the neat divisions so dear to the heart of modern Westerners. Exodus 19:6 forcefully expresses the ancient idea as it records the words of the Lord to Israel: "You will be for me a kingdom of priests and a holy nation." The "civil" words in this description are *kingdom* and *nation,* whereas the "religious" words are *priests* and *holy.* We note, however, that they are interwoven in a way that molds them into a unity. From its inception Israel is represented as a theocracy, a nation governed by a God who is king over his people.

The Book of Deuteronomy tells us that from the outset it was evident that God intended, in greater or lesser measure, to make use of human representatives in governing his people. Throughout the history of Israel the Lord would deputize certain chosen individuals to serve as prophets at his shrines, priests in his temples, and kings on his thrones. To the extent that such divinely ordained servants performed their functions *under* God rather than *instead of* God the theocracy would prosper spiritually and materially. But whenever prophet, priest, or king tried to fulfill the requirements of his office without the help or against the will of the Lord, he would court disaster for himself as well as for the nation. Such is the burden of Deuteronomy as it describes the theocratic offices.

In Deuteronomy 18:14–19 Moses envisions a series of godly prophets whose role it would be to speak forth God's word to God's people in God's name. Unlike the neighboring nations, Israel was not to give heed to sorcerers and diviners, who were detestable in the Lord's sight (18:10–12). Nor was Israel to pay attention to so-called prophets who spoke "in the name of other gods," because such presumptuous people were worthy only of death (18:20). On the contrary, God promised to raise up in and from Israel prophets like Moses himself, men and women who would speak to the people the words that God commanded them to speak. At the very beginning of the theocracy, prior to the entrance of Israel into Canaan, Moses thus establishes the importance of the prophetic ministry.

In Deuteronomy 31:9–13 Moses outlines for the priests, the sons of Levi, their role as public readers of the words of the law. It is common to view the priests of the Old Testament merely as the ones who sacrificed animals and officiated at rituals. The Bible makes clear, however, that they were also the ones who executed the very important function of reading aloud the stipulations of the Mosaic covenant in connection with frequent periodic ceremonies of renewal. In Leviticus 10:10–11 the teaching office of the priests is placed on a par with their capacity as those who are to "distinguish between the holy and the common, between the unclean and the clean." Before Israel's conquest of the promised land and at the very beginning of the theocracy, Moses thus confirms the high calling of the priestly ministry.

In Deuteronomy 17:14–20 Moses foresees the eventual emergence of a series of kings in and from Israel whose role it would be to govern the people of God wisely and well in the political arena. After pointing out the occupational hazards that pose an ever-present threat to any oriental monarchy—such as the temptations to enter into entangling alliances with foreign powers, to establish a harem, and to "accumulate large amounts of silver and gold" (17:17)—Moses calls our attention to a royal function often unnoticed by present-day students of the Bible and just as often neglected by the ancient Israelite rulers themselves. The king was to write for himself a copy of the law, read from it frequently, and follow carefully all of its stipulations. His resulting familiarity with the terms of the covenant would keep him both righteous and humble, enable him to rule justly and decisively, and guarantee him a long and prosperous reign. Although Israel would not found her monarchy until centuries after her entrance into Canaan, at the very beginning of the theocracy Moses here gives powerful witness to the divine origin and eventual significance of the kingly ministry.

The centrality of the word of God appears in sharp focus in Moses' careful discussion of the three main theocratic offices. Only as the prophets proclaimed and the priests taught and the kings absorbed and practiced the covenant stipulations would the people of Israel live in the light of God's blessings. It is extremely difficult for a governmental organization to maintain itself for long without a written constitution whose provisions the people obey either voluntarily or under compulsion. As we have already seen, in the case of Israel the Ten Commandments formed the basic body of law, the minimal covenant statement to which every Israelite was required to give allegiance. The expanded commentary (Exod. 20:22–23:33) on the Decalogue, referred to generally as "the Book of the Covenant" (24:7), spelled out in detail some of the implications of Exodus 20:2–17 and added other laws that were to be observed as well. The entire Book of Leviticus, together with large sections of Numbers and Deuteronomy, rounded out the decrees, laws, and commands by which Israel was to govern its conduct in every area of life. Without the Word of God written, Israel could scarcely have survived in the midst of the community of nations as long as it did.

It is not difficult to observe a progressive deterioration in the theocratic ideal as we follow the political development of the people of God from Sinai to Babylonia and beyond. Israel's governmental organization in the desert was simple enough. The twelve tribes assembled themselves, both literally and figuratively, around a central shrine (Num. 2). It is possible that each tribe paid for the expenses of the tabernacle one month out of the year. Solomon's later division of the land of Israel into twelve administrative districts for the purpose of providing for the expenses of his court (1 Kings 4:7, 27) would then be a reflection of the same ancient practice. The earlier and simpler organization of Israel's economy, however, continued through the period of the judges. As the rallying point of the political and religious life of the tribes, the tabernacle served to remind the people of their theocratic heritage. Never did Israel enjoy a more direct rule of God than during the centuries leading up to the foundation of the monarchy. The only rulers of the tribes were charismatic military leaders, men and women who were endowed by the Spirit of God at times of spiritual and political emergency to interpret for the people the precepts of the law, to arbitrate for them their disputes at court, and to win victories for them on the field of battle. We are not surprised to learn that, during the centuries that these judges governed Israel, Gideon's son Abimelech, the erstwhile king of Shechem, was killed almost single-handedly by a woman and that the Old Testament narrator records the story with a kind of scornful delight (Judg. 9:50–55). We could only wish that Abimelech had abided by the convictions of his father, who had earlier spoken these words to the men of Israel: "I will not rule over you, nor will my son rule over you. The LORD will rule over you" (8:23). In so saying, Gideon was doubtless voicing not only his own viewpoint but also the opinion of many of his contemporaries. They believed that it was improper and dangerous to try to interfere with God's freedom to govern his people as he so desired.

As the years came and went, however, increasing pressures favoring a more authoritarian form of government were brought to bear at the highest levels of Israel's political life. The dreary and ever-recurring cycles of willful rebellion, severe punishment, desperate petition, and divine deliverance that characterized the period of the judges (Judg. 2:10–19; Neh. 9:26–28) could not go on forever. The aged Samuel, the last of Israel's judges, was confronted with the full dimensions of the problem when the tribal elders came to him and said, "You are old, and your sons do not walk in your ways; now appoint a king to lead us, such as all the other nations have" (1 Sam. 8:5). Samuel's displeasure in the face of these remarks was relieved somewhat when the Lord informed him that it was he, not Samuel, whom the people were in the process of rejecting. The Lord then instructed Samuel to warn Israel of the serious and drastic nature of the step they were taking in their desire to adopt monarchy as their form of government. But the people held their ground and continued to press their demands for a king so that, as they said, "we will be like all the other nations, with a king to lead us and go out before us and fight our battles" (8:20). Samuel observed sadly that they had become disenchanted with their judges and that they were pressing for a more indirect rule of God over their lives (12:11–13).

The change from judgeship to kingship was not abrupt, however. While it is true that both Saul and David, the first two rulers of united Israel, are given the title "king" (1 Sam. 13:1; 2 Sam. 2:4), we must also observe that they are frequently called by the less despotic title "leader" (1 Sam. 9:16; 10:1; 13:14; 25:30) or "ruler" (2 Sam. 5:2; 6:21; 7:8; 1 Chron. 11:2; 17:7), a description of them that was a favorite of Samuel himself. Samuel anointed both Saul and David (1 Sam. 10:1; 16:13), and he may have looked upon them as transitional figures between the period of the judges and the establishment of the monarchy. Like the kings who followed them, Saul and David built royal dwellings (19:9; 2 Sam. 5:9) and led armies into battle. Like the judges who preceded them, they were men upon whom the Spirit of God came in power to enable them to perform his will (1 Sam. 10:10; 16:13).

When David's son Solomon ascended the throne of Israel in about 970 B.C., the nation experienced its first encounter with dynastic monarchy. Solomon inherited a vast empire from his father and proceeded to make its influence and resources completely subservient to his desires, which were in large measure childish if not selfish. Because of Solomon's expensive tastes it was necessary for him to tax the people heavily. After he had died and when his son Rehoboam stupidly proposed to make the burden of taxation heavier rather than lighter, the ten northern tribes revolted and seceded from the empire (1 Kings 11:42–12:24).

Despite the faults of Solomon and Rehoboam, however, the Lord blessed the southern kingdom, thereafter known as Judah, because of the enduring promises he had made to David (2 Sam. 7:8–16; Ps. 89:1–37; Isa. 55:3). With the exception of the apostate rebel queen Athaliah, all twenty of the rulers who sat on the throne in Jerusalem from Rehoboam to Zedekiah were members of the Davidic dynasty. Many of them were also reformers who were concerned for the spiritual welfare of their subjects. The northern kingdom, known as Israel after the death of Solomon, also had twenty rulers during its history. But there the similarity ends, because the kings of the north were uniformly evil and enjoyed no continuing dynasty. The Lord's description of the deplorable situation as voiced through his prophet is clear enough: "They set up kings without my consent; they choose princes without my approval" (Hos. 8:4). Samaria, the capital of Israel, fell to the Assyrians in 722 B.C. Jerusalem, the capital of Judah, was able to maintain its somewhat tenuous existence for well over a century beyond that time, but eventually and inevitably it was leveled by the Babylonians in 586. The southern kingdom was carried into exile, just as the northern kingdom had been removed from its land earlier. The Israelite theocracy thus came to an end for all practical purposes, since the sporadic attempts to reconstitute home rule in Judah during the intertestamental period were almost always made under the shadow and with the permission of Persia, Greece, or Rome.

If the sun of Israel's political glory had set, however, its spiritual splendor broke forth into a new dawn just when the Roman Empire was at the zenith of its power. One of God's choice servants had prophesied the emergence of one who, as Prophet, Priest, and King, would develop a revolutionary theocratic concept: "You, Bethlehem Ephrathah, though you are small among the clans of Judah, out of you will come for me one who will be ruler over Israel, whose origins are from of old, from ancient times" (Mic. 5:2). And as it had been written, in about 6 B.C. he came (Matt. 2:1–6). He grew into manhood, increasing all the while in wisdom and stature as well as in divine and human favor (Luke 2:52). His early preaching strikes a distinctly theocratic note: "The time has come. . . . The kingdom of God is near. Repent and believe the good news!" (Mark 1:15). His emphasis on repentance and faith, coupled with his repeated stress on the fact that his kingship is neither of nor from this world (John 18:36), highlights the spiritual dimension of his rule without belittling in the least his eventual and universal dominion in every realm.

In theocratic language borrowed from Exodus 19:5–6, Peter proclaimed to Christians of the first century and, by extension, to us as well: "You are a chosen people, a royal priesthood, a holy nation, a people belonging to God, that you may declare the praises of him who called you out of darkness into his wonderful light" (1 Peter 2:9). Similarly John referred to all who have been liberated from their sins by the blood of Christ as "a kingdom and priests to serve his God and Father" (Rev. 1:6; see also 5:10). Needless to say, however, we must not sacrifice the yet future expression of Christ's royal power to his present rule over the hearts of his people. The time will inevitably arrive when it will be possible for all the redeemed to shout: "The kingdom of the world has become the kingdom of our Lord and of his Christ, and he will reign for ever and ever" (11:15). Only then will the ultimate theocracy, the kingdom of God, be revealed in all its glory.

"Come, Lord Jesus" (Rev. 22:20).

7  Law

The law of the LORD is perfect.

Psalm 19:7

Recently in America the highest rate of increase in serious crimes has generally taken place in small towns and suburban areas. This suggests that overcrowded living conditions, poverty, and inadequate education are not the only factors that produce lawlessness. The words of Jesus to people of his time are equally true today: "What goes into a man's mouth does not make him 'unclean,' but what comes out of his mouth, that is what makes him 'unclean.' . . . The things that come out of the mouth come from the heart, and these make a man 'unclean.' For out of the heart come evil thoughts, murder, adultery, sexual immorality, theft, false testimony, slander. These are what make a man 'unclean'; but eating with unwashed hands does not make him 'unclean' " (Matt. 15:11, 18–20).

In other words, disrespect for law has more to do with internal attitudes than with external environments. This does not mean that Christians should not labor with might and main for the amelioration of sordid social conditions and the alleviation of human misery and suffering. It means simply that the search for solutions to the problem of rebellion in church and state must probe deeply into the heart. Nor are superficial solutions the answer, either externally or internally. As it does not help people who are accustomed to slum dwellings to resettle them in brand-new apartment buildings, which they will quickly turn into slums, so also it is of no use to exorcise a demon from a man if we leave the resulting void unfilled, thereby permitting a return of the demon with seven of his wicked associates and providing a situation in which "the final condition of that man is worse than the first" (Luke 11:26). The Old Testament prophets also understood clearly that easy answers to the problems raised by human sin were no answers at all: "Can the Ethiopian change his skin or the leopard its spots? Neither can you do good who are accustomed to doing evil" (Jer. 13:23).

Jeremiah assumed, of course, that his fellow Israelites knew the difference between good and evil. He had a perfect right to assume such knowledge on their part because the law of Moses had been in effect for centuries as the basic standard of conduct for God's people, regulating every area of their lives. The one true God, the sovereign Creator and Lord of the universe, had chosen, out of all the nations, one people whose mission it was to receive and preserve his word and, ultimately, proclaim it to all who would listen. In solemn confirmation of his choice he had established a covenant with the fledgling Israelite nation at Mount Sinai and had graciously committed himself to them as the divine King of their theocratic form of government. At the same time God had imposed on his people rules of conduct as embodied in the covenant stipulations. The law, which is the term by which these rules are best known, was intended not only to represent the demands of a holy God upon a sinful people but also to make the theocratic system workable throughout Israel's history. As the intention of the Sinaitic covenant can be understood only in terms of divine imposition of authority coupled with glad and obedient response on the part of God's people, so also must we view the law in a similar light. It can thus be seen that the law, as the most important single aspect of the covenant and in a certain sense synonymous with it, lies near the heart of Old Testament teaching.

Our understanding of the divine origin of the Mosaic law should not be permitted to blind us to the fact that it did not make its appearance in a cultural vacuum. Almost a hundred years ago the cuneiform Code of Hammurapi was discovered in Persia in the ruins of the old Elamite capital of Susa. It dates from the eighteenth century B.C., hundreds of years before Moses was born. Since its discovery, three separate and still more ancient cuneiform law codes have come to light. All of these legal materials demonstrate conclusively that much of what we read in the stipulations of the law of Moses, in many cases with certain modifications to be sure, was already common currency in the ancient Near East by the time Moses and his compatriots arrived at Sinai. A recognition of this undeniable historical fact, however, does not in itself undercut either our belief in the inspiration of Scripture or the uniqueness of the Old Testament contribution to moral legislation. The Mosaic law simply becomes another illustration of the condescension of God in utilizing literary forms and legal customs as the most suitable vehicles available for revealing his purposes to his children in the most easily understandable and clearly comprehensible manner.

It is helpful to distinguish between two major literary forms used by Moses in the legislative portions of his writings. One, the so-called casuistic style, is the more common of the two and is characteristic also of extrabiblical cuneiform law generally. Its structure is easily recognized: "If a man does so-and-so, then such-and-such will be the penalty." Two examples from the Book of the Covenant (Exod. 20:22–23:33) will suffice: "If a man steals an ox or a sheep and slaughters it or sells it, he must pay back five head of cattle for the ox and four sheep for the sheep" (22:1). "If a man borrows an animal from his neighbor and it is injured or dies while the owner is not present, he must make restitution" (22:14). That the Mosaic legislation shares the casuistic literary form with cuneiform law can be seen, for example, from a comparison with the very first section of the legal stipulations in the Code of Hammurapi: "If a freeman has accused another freeman and has hurled a charge of murder against him but has not convicted him, his accuser shall be executed."

The other major literary category discernible in the law of Moses is the so-called apodictic type. It would be overstating the case to insist that no examples of this form are found outside the Bible in ancient times. We can affirm, however, that it stands out as Israel's characteristic and distinctive contribution in the history of law codes and that for all practical purposes it remains a unique feature of the Mosaic legislation. The apodictic legal formula is stated in terms of a categorical imperative: "You shall/shall not do so-and-so." Many stipulations of this kind are sprinkled throughout the laws of Moses, but the best known and most outstanding example of apodictic legislation in the entire Old Testament is the Ten Commandments (Exod. 20:2–17; Deut. 5:6–21). We commented on certain aspects of their literary form and context in connection with our discussion of the Sinaitic covenant in chapter 5. We shall now investigate their contents more closely.

Some time ago, the Oklahoma State Pardon and Parole Board ruled that inmates who wanted to be released from the state prison in McAlester had to make a sincere effort to learn the Ten Commandments by heart. Such a commendable requirement, however, is rare indeed in our day. We are told that the Decalogue was a rigid code intended only for the primitive people of Israel, and that our task today is to develop ethical and moral standards that are less absolute and more liberal and that will therefore appeal to modern sophisticates. We are also told that the Ten Commandments are neither more nor less than a series of "don'ts" and that people today are willing to respond only to overtures expressed in a positive way. The modern mood therefore stamps the Ten Commandments as being completely passé. Besides, everything is relative anyway, is it not?

The Christian must take issue with any such negative evaluation of the Ten Commandments. For one thing, the New Testament letters often quote from them (see for example Rom. 13:9; James 2:11), and never in a way leading to the conclusion that we may simply dismiss them out of hand. Their primary reference to Israel (Exod. 20:2) should not blind us to their value for us as well, and indeed for the whole human race. For another thing, in the Sermon on the Mount Jesus himself quoted two of the Ten Commandments and reinforced their importance by affirming that one could disobey them not only by outward action but also through inner motivation (Matt. 5:21–30). Furthermore, Christ summed up the basic thrust of the Decalogue as love for God and love for one's neighbor (Mark 12:28–31), and love is surely the purest and most positive of all emotions (see also Rom. 13:8–10). That the form of the Ten Commandments is basically negative no one would doubt, but to conclude on that account that their orientation is also basically negative is to contradict the facts of the case.

As the most fundamental summary of the Mosaic law, the Decalogue describes our responsibilities toward God as well as our proper relationships toward our fellow human beings, as Jesus so clearly taught in the above-mentioned passages. The first four commandments are decidedly religious in emphasis and close with a positive injunction: "Remember the Sabbath day by keeping it holy" (Exod. 20:8). The last six commandments stress moral and ethical relationships and begin with a positive injunction: "Honor your father and your mother" (20:12). As we now examine each of the Ten Commandments in turn, we will attempt to understand what they meant for the people to whom they were first proclaimed and then to determine what they should mean for us today.

"You shall have no other gods before me" (Exod. 20:3). Israel was to have no other objects of worship in preference to, or in addition to, or in hostility against, the one true God. The people were to be completely single-minded in their worship. Jesus affirmed the same general principle in Matthew 6:24: "No one can serve two masters. Either he will hate the one and love the other, or he will be devoted to the one and despise the other. You cannot serve both God and Money" (see also Luke 16:13). Refusal to obey the first commandment can have disastrous consequences in other areas of life as well. In a different but related context, James reminds us that "a double-minded man" is "unstable in all he does" (James 1:8). Competing gods that vie for our allegiance today may differ in many respects from those that tempted ancient Israel, but single-mindedness is nevertheless a goal that still eludes countless Christians. Like the Pharisees of Jesus' day (Luke 16:14), many of us at times tend to ensconce material wealth in the uppermost throne room of our hearts, to give just one example.

"You shall not make for yourself an idol" (Exod. 20:4). At first glance the second commandment appears to be simply another way of stating the prohibition expressed in the first commandment. We may observe a certain progression here, however. The first commandment affirms that there is only one God worthy of his people's worship, while the second specifies the main source of temptation that could lead to the breaking of the first. Idolatry—worshiping gods made in the images of human beings and lesser creatures—was the primary obstacle to the development of Israel's spiritual life from the earliest times down to the period of the exile. The Book of the Covenant recognized its dangers from the outset: "Do not make any gods to be alongside me; do not make for yourselves gods of silver or gods of gold" (20:23). Because he is a sovereign God, the Lord is also "a jealous God" (20:5) who brooks no rivals. Indeed, his very name is "Jealous" (34:14). Furthermore, because "God is spirit" (John 4:24) and therefore has no form, to attempt to picture him in a tangible or plastic way is to portray him inaccurately and therefore is unworthy (Deut. 4:12–19). Although today we are not tempted by the grosser forms of pagan worship that plagued ancient Israel, we have our own idols. To use an expression made popular by J. B. Phillips, our God is often too small. Every time we try to squeeze God into preconceived theological molds we think in terms of a deity that is something other, and therefore less, than the God and Father of our Lord Jesus Christ. The Lord is greater than our fondest imaginings, and it is appropriate to give him our worship only in terms of the ways in which he is described in the Scriptures themselves. Nor will he accept our worship if it is based on improper motivation or if it springs from unclean hearts. "Put to death, therefore, whatever belongs to your earthly nature: sexual immorality, impurity, lust, evil desires and greed, which is idolatry" (Col. 3:5).

"You shall not misuse the name of the LORD your God" (Exod. 20:7). The best commentary on the third commandment is Leviticus 19:12: "Do not swear falsely by my name and so profane the name of your God. I am the LORD." In the ancient Semitic world, taking an oath in a court of law was characteristically performed in the presence of the image of a god, and the oath itself was pronounced in the name of that god. In Israel, of course, there could be no question of oath-taking before an image of the Lord because of the prohibition found in the second commandment. Nevertheless, even apart from formal court procedure it was common practice for Israelites and, on occasion, non-Israelites (see 1 Kings 17:1, 12) to swear by the name of the Lord in order to confirm the truth of their assertions. It is clear, then, that the third commandment is more an injunction against perjury than against profanity. In addition, however, it was believed in ancient times that to manipulate a name in any way was also to control, at least to some extent, the person who bore that name. To pronounce the name of a god, therefore, was to influence that god somewhat, whether for good or for evil. Swearing by the name of the one true God is thus always a hazardous proposition. This fact should serve to remind us of the solemnity of the oath taken by witnesses in our modern courts, an oath that concludes with the affirmation: "So help me God." To be aware of the ever-present danger of showing disrespect for God's name is to take seriously Christ's commentary on the third commandment: "Do not swear at all: either by heaven, for it is God's throne; or by the earth, for it is his footstool; or by Jerusalem, for it is the city of the Great King. . . . Simply let your 'Yes' be 'Yes,' and your 'No,' 'No' " (Matt. 5:34–35, 37).

"Remember the Sabbath day by keeping it holy" (Exod. 20:8). One day in seven was to be set aside as holy to the Lord, and that for at least three reasons: (1) in celebration of the original creation of the universe (20:11), (2) in commemoration of past enslavement and subsequent redemption from Egyptian bondage (Deut. 5:15), and (3) in common-sense recognition of the need for periodic rest (Exod. 23:12). The temptation to use the Sabbath day for unworthy purposes is not only a modern attraction; throughout Israel's history people could be found who were unable to confine their personal and often selfish interests and activities to six days of the week (Amos 8:4–6). But Sabbath observance took on even greater significance for the perceptive Israelite who realized that just as the rainbow was the sign of the Noahic covenant, and just as circumcision was the sign of the Abrahamic covenant, so also was keeping the Sabbath not only a part of the Mosaic covenant itself but also a sign of that divinely established relationship (Exod. 31:12–17). Likewise the Christian modification of the Sabbath, which we now observe on the first rather than the seventh day of the week in recognition of the resurrection of Christ, reminds us that Jesus died for us on the eve of a typical Jewish Sabbath, that he spent that same Sabbath in a tomb outside the walls of Jerusalem, that he arose from the dead early the following morning, and that therefore every Sunday gives us another opportunity to celebrate the new birth that we enjoy in him, to commemorate our release from the slavery of sin, to look forward to our final eschatological rest at the time of our own guaranteed resurrection, and to rejoice in the innumerable blessings of the new covenant in his blood.

"Honor your father and your mother" (Exod. 20:12). We will devote proportionately less space to each of the six ethical commandments than we did to each of the four religious commandments in accordance with the example set by the Decalogue itself. The fifth commandment forms an appropriate transition between the two groups since, according to Leviticus 19:32, honoring the older person and fearing the Lord are parallel obligations. As the first four commandments remind us to give to God the proper respect, so also does the fifth enjoin us to do the same for our parents, who are God's delegates for the supervision and training of his younger children. Paul prefaced his citation of the fifth commandment by admonishing all of us to obey our parents "in the Lord, for this is right" (Eph. 6:1).

"You shall not murder" (Exod. 20:13). The sixth commandment follows somewhat logically on the preceding one since the death penalty could be inflicted for striking one's father or mother (21:15). It would appear that all crimes of violence are summed up in the terse words of the sixth commandment, because Christ indicated that anger and insult and ridicule are tantamount to murder (Matt. 5:21–22). Human life, because made in the image of God, is precious, and the penalties for shedding human blood are severe and, in many cases, ultimate (Gen. 9:6).

"You shall not commit adultery" (Exod. 20:14). Both the taking of another man's life and the taking of another man's wife were punishable by death, and in the latter case the adulteress shared the same extreme penalty (Lev. 20:10). The family was a basic and sacred unit in ancient times (Gen. 2:24), and nothing was to be permitted to disturb or disrupt its sanctity. Although polygamy was sometimes practiced, the Bible never condones it. Indeed, in certain important instances the Bible sternly warns against it (see, for example, Deut. 17:17). In any event, the Christian today must be guided by the affirmation of our Lord, who stated that the lustful look is a sign of an adulterous heart (Matt. 5:28).

"You shall not steal" (Exod. 20:15). The observation that committing adultery with another man's wife is a form of theft serves to tie the eighth commandment closely to the seventh. In more ancient and somewhat less complex civilizations than our own, the definition of thievery and the identification of thieves were relatively simple and routine. Today, however, theft takes on much more sophisticated forms such as cheating on examinations, labor slowdowns, price-fixing arrangements, making false statements on income-tax reports, stealing of company secrets, and planned obsolescence. This commandment illustrates perhaps more clearly than any other how infinitely devious the human heart is (see Jer. 17:9).

"You shall not give false testimony" (Exod. 20:16). Human depravity might well be expected to manifest itself on the witness stand in court trials, and for that reason more than one witness was required in capital punishment cases since reputations and ultimately lives were at stake (Deut. 17:6; 1 Kings 21:9–14). False witness is, in effect, the theft of an individual's reputation, a fact that helps to explain the position of the ninth commandment in the Decalogue. Leviticus 19:11 brings together three related injunctions and serves to illustrate this point: "Do not steal. Do not lie. Do not deceive one another." It can thus be seen that falsehood in speech is equivalent in value to falsehood in action.

"You shall not covet" (Exod. 20:17). The tenth and final commandment prepared the way for Christ's emphasis in the Sermon on the Mount on inner motivation as a prelude to external action (Matt. 5:21, 22, 27, 28). Although the other nine commandments do not exclude entirely the inward aspects of moral behavior, the tenth makes such aspects explicit. As we have already stated more than once, Jesus summed up the Decalogue in a similar way by describing its total impact in terms of love. If we love, we will not covet, so that in the most profound of senses "love is the fulfillment of the law" (Rom. 13:10).

Christians today find it difficult to determine just how they should evaluate the law of Moses, whether as it is set forth in capsule form in the Ten Commandments or as it is found in its more expanded expressions. Is the law good, or is it evil? Is it to be viewed negatively or positively? Are we correct in equating the Old Testament with law and death and the New Testament with grace and life?

Our answers to these questions must be based on the Scriptures themselves, of course. On the one hand, Paul called the law "holy" (Rom. 7:12) and listed it among the blessings enjoyed by his fellow Israelites (9:4). Such an evaluation of the law accords well with that found in the Old Testament itself (Ps. 19:7–11; Deut. 4:8). In fact the longest chapter in the Bible, Psalm 119, is a hymn praising the law of God. On the other hand, however, Paul also wrote about "the curse of the law" (Gal. 3:13).

The basic solution to this dilemma would seem to be to face the fact that positive and negative evaluations of the law are both correct. When viewed from the Old Testament perspective, the law was one of God's choicest gifts of grace to his people, serving as their custodian until Christ came (Gal. 3:23–24). Whenever the law was looked upon as a means of salvation, however, the New Testament writers categorically denied its significance (2:15–16). But the law can assist believers to grow in grace after their conversion. We who have faith in Jesus as the Christ have learned what it means to love God (1 John 5:1–2) and have experienced the fact that "his commands are not burdensome" (5:3).

8  Sacrifice

> I will sacrifice . . . bulls and goats.
>
> Psalm 66:15

Once upon a time a pig and a chicken were strolling together down a dusty country road. Coming upon a rustic little church, they noticed the wording on the freshly lettered sign outside: Ham and Eggs Breakfast Tomorrow Morning.

Said the chicken to the pig: "I have an excellent idea. Let's both go in and make a contribution."

Said the pig to the chicken: "Not on your life. For you it would be a contribution, but for me it would be a sacrifice."

An old and corny joke, to be sure. Nevertheless, it illustrates the fact that sacrifice is a serious and costly matter. There is, after all, an important difference between a contribution and a sacrifice. One may make a contribution, whether in time or talent or treasure or in any of a number of other ways, without experiencing too much inconvenience. One cannot make a sacrifice, however, without counting the cost either sooner or later. A contribution demands only minimal involvement. A sacrifice is a gift of life.

When we begin to discuss sacrifice in the religious sense generally and in the biblical sense specifically, we immediately realize that it takes on an even more serious and somber complexion. The one true God, sovereign over the universe, chose to relate himself to his people by means of a series of covenants. The greatest of the Old Testament compacts, the Sinaitic or Mosaic covenant, became embodied in a theocratic form of government based on the law of Moses. In the preceding chapter we examined the nonceremonial aspects of that law as they are summarized in the Ten Commandments. We now turn our attention to the most important of the ceremonial emphases of the law that the Bible recognizes as being contained in the sacrificial system of Mosaism. When viewed against such a background, the subject of sacrifice is seen to be one of the great themes of the Old Testament.

As we have already indicated in connection with certain other ancient Israelite customs and practices, so we can also demonstrate that with respect to sacrificial procedures God's people did not live entirely apart from their neighbors. Israel shared a number of ritual customs and accessories with other peoples in the Near East, and it is not always easy to determine in which direction the borrowing lay. We must be willing to admit from the outset, as the Bible itself does, that when the Israelites arrived in Canaan the native inhabitants had already possessed for centuries a full-fledged and elaborate cult together with all the appurtenances necessary to maintain its proper observance. In revealing to Moses the details of the establishment of Israel's sacrificial system, God made use of some of the unobjectionable features of Near Eastern ritual, condemned certain aspects that were obscene or blasphemous or hopelessly pagan, and added a number of unique and distinctive contributions of his own gracious provision. Only by recognizing the presence of such similarities and differences can we arrive at a full-orbed and proper understanding of sacrifice in Israel. Perhaps a few examples will help to clarify the somewhat complicated situation just described.

In a dedicatory inscription written in honor of his goddess, King Yehawmilk of Byblos mentions an altar of bronze that he had made for her, reminiscent of "the bronze altar before the LORD" (1 Kings 8:64). King Solomon's many marriages to foreign wives resulted in the importation into Israel of numerous pagan cultic practices, many of which had their purified counterparts in the divinely authorized Israelite religion. Solomon acceded to his wives' demands by constructing places of worship where the ladies of the court were then able to burn incense and offer sacrifices to their gods (11:7–8). The classic example of the similarities between Canaanite and Israelite sacrificial procedure is the description of the contest on Mount Carmel between Elijah on the one hand and the prophets of Baal and prophets of Asherah on the other (see especially 18:19–33). Israel also shared her sacrificial terminology with her neighbors, for we read of freewill offerings (see Lev. 7:16) in Babylonian texts and of grain offerings (see 7:37) in Phoenician inscriptions. The ancient idea that sacrificial offerings served as food for the gods (see Deut. 32:37–38) is found in the Ugaritic Aqhat epic, and a modification of the belief as imputed to the Lord is found in a metaphorical context in Ezekiel 44:6–7.

Such comparisons can scarcely be maintained, however, when we move from general to more specific parallels. For example, as far as we are able to tell, the elaborate manipulation of sacrificial blood by the priests of Israel had no counterpart in the ritual of her pagan neighbors, who did little more than allow the blood to run into a catch basin. Blood did not receive the same attention or assume the same importance in other nations that it did in Israel. Furthermore, certain sacrificial practices were roundly condemned by the Old Testament, either because they were immoral or simply because they were characteristically foreign. Human sacrifice, for example, which was very common among Israel's neighbors (see 2 Kings 3:26–27), is expressly prohibited to the people of God (Lev. 18:21; Jer. 7:31). Against such a background the story of Jephthah's terrible vow becomes all the more stark (Judg. 11:30–40). Finally, the recent archeological revelation that the sacrifice of honey was a Canaanite ritual custom yields a sufficient explanation for the prohibition described in Leviticus 2:11.

Enough has been said already in this chapter to emphasize the fact that one of the basic principles of sacrifice involves the giving of life or the products of one's livelihood to one's god or gods. Such a principle within the scope of ancient pagan religion is brought out most vividly in the hideous practice of the sacrifice of human beings. The God of Israel condemned that method of sacrifice for obvious moral and humane reasons. In its place Israelites were to offer nonhuman, and particularly animal, sacrifices. The reason for the frequency of animal sacrificial practice in non-Israelite cultures may be somewhat difficult to ascertain, but in Israel the ceremony doubtless reflects the other basic principle underlying biblical sacrifice: the substituting of one life for another. The Israelites could not offer their own lives or the lives of any other human beings to the one true God. They therefore presented the life of an animal as a substitute and so fulfilled their sacrificial obligations.

The tension-filled story of Abraham and Isaac in Genesis 22 dramatically illustrates the principles of the gift of life and the substitution of life. God said to Abraham, "Take your son, your only son, Isaac, whom you love, and . . . sacrifice him . . . as a burnt offering" (v. 2). The way in which the proposed sacrifice is described—"your son . . . your only son . . . Isaac . . . whom you love"—makes it evident that Abraham was being required to present as a gift to God the life that was nearest and dearest to him. But having demonstrated his willingness to obey God's command to the letter, Abraham witnessed the gracious application of the principle of the substitution of life: "Abraham looked up and there in a thicket he saw a ram caught by its horns. He went over and took the ram and sacrificed it as a burnt offering instead of his son" (v. 13). Isaac, the gift of life, was to have been the burnt offering, but the ram, the substituted life, became the offering in his place.

As a result of Abraham's unquestioning obedience toward and unswerving faith in God, the Lord promised to reward him, as he himself said: "Because you have done this and have not withheld your son, your only son, I will surely bless you" (vv. 16–17).

By reproducing a portion of the wording of this passage in a Christian context, Paul recognized in Isaac a type of Jesus Christ: "He who did not spare his own Son, but gave him up for us all— how will he not also, along with him, graciously give us all things?" (Rom. 8:32).

Needless to say, many such fruitful comparisons can easily be made between the sacrificial system of Mosaism and the supreme, once-for-all, final sacrifice of the Lord Jesus. As we turn now to the process of sacrifice as it is described in the Old Testament, we shall attempt to note pertinent parallels with the New Testament in each step of the procedure. A characteristic passage that outlines most of the stages in the sacrificial ritual is found in Exodus 29, which portrays in detail the ceremony used to consecrate Aaron and his sons as priests. In our examination of this chapter we shall concentrate on the first fourteen verses only and highlight those phrases that best illustrate the basic pattern of sacrificial procedure as the Old Testament knows it elsewhere as well.

In the first place Moses was to select the proper animals for the solemn purpose at hand: "Take a young bull and two rams without defect" (29:1). The youthful nature of the animals stresses the fact that they were to be offered when they had reached the prime of life. In the case of the Passover Feast the sacrifice was to be a year-old sheep or goat (12:5), whereas sacrificial bulls were apparently to be three years old (1 Sam. 1:24). But in addition to being prime with respect to age, the offered animal was to be perfect with respect to condition. With but rare exceptions no animal disfigured by a blemish of any kind was worthy of being sacrificed to the Lord. The animal's perfection in age and condition symbolized the wholehearted devotion of the offerers as they presented their gifts of life to God, the spotless substitute life reminding them, by contrast, of their own impurities.

The fourth Song of the Suffering Servant (Isa. 52:13–53:12) hints at the importance of this aspect of biblical sacrificial procedure. The voluntary sufferer, who "bore the sin of many" (53:12), is pictured figuratively as a lamb that is led "to the slaughter" (53:7). His spotless character is mirrored in the observation that "he had done no violence, nor was any deceit in his mouth" (53:9). He was, indeed, the Lord's "righteous servant" (53:11). As the ultimate New Testament fulfillment of Isaiah's Suffering Servant concept (see, for example, Acts 8:32–35), Jesus was a perfect lamb of sacrifice (1 Cor. 5:7) with respect to both age and condition. It is often claimed today that a man reaches his prime of life between the ages of thirty and thirty-five, and the chronology of the New Testament leads us to the conclusion that Christ was crucified when he was in his early thirties. Although we would not overemphasize this particular parallel, recognizing that it could be merely coincidental, the purity of Christ throughout his life and at the time of his death is beyond question (Heb. 4:14–15). Peter makes the comparison explicit: "You know that it was not with perishable things such as silver or gold that you were redeemed from the empty way of life handed down to you from your forefathers, but with the precious blood of Christ, a lamb without blemish or defect" (1 Peter 1:18–19). Jesus, the perfect sacrifice, fulfilled for all time the expectations of the ancient Israelite believer as he brought to the Lord his youthful and spotless animal.

The second step in the Old Testament sacrificial process was the laying on of hands: "Bring the bull to the front of the Tent of Meeting, and Aaron and his sons shall lay their hands on its head" (Exod. 29:10). Such an action symbolized the transfer of something from subject to object. Examples of this frequent and widespread practice in many kinds of situations are numerous. Jacob symbolically bestowed his blessing upon the two sons of Joseph by putting his hands on their heads (Gen. 48:14–16). A blasphemer could be stoned by the congregation of Israel only after all who had heard his curses had witnessed to their embarrassment and humiliation by laying their hands on his head (Lev. 24:14). Moses invested Joshua with some of his own authority and filled him with the spirit of wisdom by laying his hands on him (Num. 27:18–23; Deut. 34:9). Ceremonies of ordination in the life of the church from the first century until now have gained their sanctity and character as they have reflected such Old Testament prototypes.

Most significant for a proper understanding of the laying on of hands during the sacrificial ritual is the account of the sending away of a live goat on the day of atonement. The high priest Aaron is to "lay both hands on the head of the live goat and confess over it all the wickedness and rebellion of the Israelites—all their sins—and put them on the goat's head. He shall send the goat away into the desert in the care of a man appointed for the task. The goat will carry on itself all their sins to a solitary place" (Lev. 16:21–22). It is obvious that the laying on of hands here involves the symbolic transfer of sin from the offerer to the sacrifice. Likewise it is said of Isaiah's Suffering Servant that "the LORD has laid on him the iniquity of us all" (Isa. 53:6). With inspired insight Peter drew out the full implications of the prophet's vision by referring it to Christ: "He himself bore our sins in his body on the tree, so that we might die to sins and live for righteousness" (1 Peter 2:24). The Father laid our sins upon his Son, who was "handed over . . . by God's set purpose and foreknowledge" (Acts 2:23).

The third step in Old Testament sacrificial procedure was the slaying of the animal: "Slaughter it in the LORD's presence" (Exod. 29:11). The act of slaughter constituted the central and most climactic scene of the entire drama. It symbolized the profound truth that sinners are worthy of death. It also proclaimed the dictum that a divinely ordained substitute is acceptable in the eyes of God. The location of the altar of burnt offering in the center of the forecourt of the tabernacle complex also testifies to the supreme significance attached to this aspect of the sacrificial process.

Like a lamb that is led "to the slaughter" (Isa. 53:7), the Suffering Servant "poured out his life unto death" (53:12) and thus "was cut off from the land of the living" (53:8). As a vicarious and therefore innocent sacrifice, "he was pierced for our transgressions, he was crushed for our iniquities" (53:5), "he bore the sin of many" (53:12). All of these descriptions apply to Jesus

Christ, as the New Testament writers recognized (see, for example, Rom. 4:25; 1 Cor. 15:3; Heb. 9:28). As the slaughter of the animal was central in the Old Testament process of sacrifice, so also is the crucifixion of our Lord pivotal in the New Testament proclamation of salvation. The authors of the Gospels devoted far more attention to the events of the last few days of Jesus' life than to any other comparable period of his earthly ministry. Paul's intellect and emotions were thoroughly captivated by his understanding of the absolute necessity and the undoubted centrality of the Savior's death. His search for the ultimate message to be preached at Corinth came to an end when he declared, "I resolved to know nothing while I was with you except Jesus Christ and him crucified" (1 Cor. 2:2). His quest for a ground of boasting outside himself was terminated when he asserted, "May I never boast except in the cross of our Lord Jesus Christ" (Gal. 6:14). That cross was the sacrificial altar on which Jesus died for us (Phil. 2:8).

The priestly manipulation of the animal's blood constituted the fourth step in the Old Testament process of sacrifice: "Take some of the bull's blood and put it on the horns of the altar with your finger, and pour out the rest of it at the base of the altar" (Exod. 29:12). The importance assigned to the blood and the elaborate procedures that its use entailed have been distinctively biblical emphases from the earliest periods. The pouring of blood on the altar symbolized the forgiveness of sins, as Leviticus 17:11 most clearly indicates: "The life of a creature is in the blood, and I have given it to you to make atonement for yourselves on the altar; it is the blood that makes atonement for one's life." In fact, hardly had the Book of Leviticus begun before the connection between blood and atonement had been made (1:4–5). The application of blood thus coincides with the cancellation of sin in the act technically known as *expiation.* Obliterating the stain of sin and thereby removing it from the sight of God is tantamount to forgiveness, as Jeremiah 18:23 teaches: "Do not forgive their crimes or blot out their sins from your sight." Throughout the Old Testament period the blood of the sacrificed animal was the divinely appointed agent that symbolized the removal of sin.

Although the Song of the Suffering Servant does not mention sacrificial blood in so many words, the idea itself may have been implicit in the mind of the author when he wrote that "by his wounds we are healed" (Isa. 53:5). The stroke of the whip caused the blood to flow, and it is against the backdrop of such a context that 1 Peter 2:24 applies the verse from Isaiah to the finished work of Christ. At any rate, the New Testament frequently emphasizes the fact that the sins of Christians have been washed away by means of the blood of Jesus. Entirely typical is 1 John 1:7: "The blood of Jesus, his Son, purifies us from all sin." The significance for the Christian of many of the concepts involved in the meaning of sacrificial blood is sharply drawn in Romans 3:23–25: "All have sinned and fall short of the glory of God, and are justified freely by his grace through the redemption that came by Christ Jesus. God presented him as a sacrifice of atonement, through faith in his blood."

One might well suppose that slaying an animal and pouring out its blood would have concluded the sacrificial process. After all, what more needs to be done after sin has been forgiven? The fifth and final stage in the procedure, however, reminds us that sacrifice has as its purpose not only expiation but also consecration: "Take all the fat around the inner parts, the covering of the liver, and both kidneys with the fat on them, and burn them on the altar" (Exod. 29:13). Such burning of certain parts of the animal was intended not to destroy but to sublimate, to produce a more refined substance that would delight the heart of God: "It is a burnt offering to the LORD, a pleasing aroma, an offering made to the LORD by fire" (29:18). The Old Testament process of sacrifice was thus concluded only after the worshiper had symbolized his willingness to consecrate himself to God by offering to him specified portions of the animal that he had brought to the altar.

The voluntary and vicarious sacrifice of Isaiah's Suffering Servant was one glorious act of consecration. As such, it pleased the heart of God in a way that is perhaps best reflected in the words of Ephesians 5:2: "Christ loved us and gave himself up for us as a fragrant offering and sacrifice to God." Our lives are to be bound up with that of Christ in specific acts of consecration because God "always leads us in triumphal procession in Christ and through us spreads everywhere the fragrance of the knowledge of him" (2 Cor. 2:14). Although we may never be summoned to lay down our lives for the Lord, consecration should always be for us a joyful surrender of all that we are and have "as living sacrifices, holy and pleasing to God" (Rom. 12:1), which is the least we can give to him who became the final sacrifice of atonement for our sins.

9

Trust in the LORD with all your heart.

Proverbs 3:5

In the King James Version of the Old Testament, the word *faith* appears only in Deuteronomy 32:20 and Habakkuk 2:4. Recent English translations, from the American Standard Version and onward, have tended to prefer renderings such as "faithfulness" instead of "faith" in the Deuteronomy passage. Considerations of tradition and theology have preserved the older translation in Habakkuk 2:4, although even in this case the alternate possibility is suggested as a secondary and marginal reading in many modern versions. One might be tempted to conclude, therefore, that faith was unimportant or even nonexistent in the religious experience of ancient Israel.

Such is clearly not the case, however. The rarity of the word *faith* is more than compensated for by the frequency of synonymous or related concepts, such as *trust, belief, commitment,* and the like. The Old Testament is full of accounts of men and women who believed in God, who committed their lives to him, who depended on him in times of victory and joy as well as in times of defeat and sorrow. Whereas the word *faith* may be one of the least common terms in the Old Testament, the idea of faith is surely one of the central emphases of the Old Testament revelation.

With respect to its constituent elements, faith is both subjective and objective, both an attitude and an action, both believing and receiving. As an attitude, true faith may be described as complete dependence on a dependable and trustworthy God. The Davidic Psalms reflect often on the indispensable nature of such confident and unswerving faith. Psalm 26:1, for example, expresses a testimony that should characterize every believer: "I have trusted in the LORD without wavering." In 18:2 God is portrayed as a mighty and impregnable fortress in whom his children may take refuge, while 37:3–5, 7 constitutes a passage in which the many-sided character of vital faith is stressed by means of a series of admonitions: "Trust in the LORD. . . . Delight yourself in the LORD. . . . Commit your way to the LORD. . . . Be still before the LORD." Faith in the sense of dependence on and trust in God was thus a common emphasis in the lives of Old Testament believers.

But there is also a negative side to the coin of faith. After urging his readers to place their complete trust in the Lord, the writer of Proverbs 3:5 gives this advice: "Lean not on your own understanding." Faith is the opposite of arrogant self-confidence. As we should always seek the Lord's counsel because "he who trusts in the LORD will prosper" (28:25), so also should we avoid relying on our own wisdom because "he who trusts in himself is a fool" (28:26). Neither should we trust in our own righteousness (Ezek. 33:13), because in the light of God's purity and holiness "all our righteous acts are like filthy rags" (Isa. 64:6). The Lord, and not one's own insights or powers, is the proper object of faith (Hos. 10:12).

But the ancient Israelites were often tempted to turn their faith in other directions. Throughout most of its history the divided kingdom was relatively weak politically. Both Israel and Judah tended, therefore, to forge military alliances with other weak nations in order to form common fronts against their more powerful neighbors. Isaiah 30:1–18 is one of many Old Testament passages that typify Judah's inclination to seek assistance from Egypt. Through a succession of sad experiences, however, Judah eventually learned the futility of "depending on Egypt, that splintered reed of a staff, which pierces a man's hand and wounds him if he leans on it" (36:6). It was only dependence on God that could deliver his people, as the Holy One of Israel himself assured them: "In repentance and rest is your salvation, in quietness and trust is your strength" (30:15).

Religion and politics may not mix well in our own day, but, as we already noted in chapter 6, in ancient times they were inseparable. King Ahaz's frantic deputation to Assyria for help against his northern enemies resulted eventually in the construction of a pagan altar within the temple precincts in Jerusalem (2 Kings 16:5–16). Such a specific action was, of course, merely a reflection of Ahaz's general practice of worshiping false and foreign gods (16:2–4). Partly because of the apostasy of so many of the kings of Israel and Judah and partly because of the tendency of the people to follow the line of least resistance by emulating their rulers, the prophets continually found it necessary to issue stern warnings against those "who trust in idols, who say to images, 'You are our gods' " (Isa. 42:17). They delighted in ridiculing both the images and those who placed their confidence in them: "He who makes it trusts in his own creation; he makes idols that cannot speak" (Hab. 2:18).

It can be seen, then, that the Old Testament is careful to point out the unworthy character of all objects of faith other than the Lord himself. Only in the one true God does faith find a trustworthy refuge. Nor is the choice of a resting place for one's confidence a relative matter. The prophets saw clearly the seriousness of the issue by declaring its outcome in terms of black and white: "Cursed is the one who trusts in man, who depends on flesh for his strength and whose heart turns away from the LORD. . . . But blessed is the man who trusts in the LORD, whose confidence is in him" (Jer. 17:5, 7).

As we have already observed, however, faith is of little value when maintained merely as an attitude of the heart. We must always be willing to demonstrate the vitality of our faith by acting on the basis of what we believe. The New Testament expresses this truth in classical form: "As the body without the spirit is dead, so faith without deeds is dead" (James 2:26). But the Old Testament is not without examples of courageous acts of faith that reflect the believer's response to "the righteous acts of the LORD" (Mic. 6:5). Indeed, Hebrews 11 has brought together in one chapter certain important attitudes that characterized and events that challenged the faith of a number of ancient worthies. In the form of a literary hall of fame the chapter portrays for the mind's eye a historical mural that begins with the life of Abel and ends with the careers of Samuel and the prophets. With deft strokes the author has sketched each individual panel in a manner that is worthy of our closest attention.

The name of Abel is the first to appear in the roll call of the faithful found in Hebrews 11. The writer states: "By faith Abel offered God a better sacrifice than Cain did" (11:4). Much has been made of the fact that Abel's was a blood sacrifice but Cain's was bloodless, and that therefore the Lord "looked with favor on Abel and his offering, but on Cain and his offering he did not look with favor" (Gen. 4:4–5). If it be true, however, as we attempted to show in chapter 8, that sacrifice in the broadest sense is the gift to God of whatever constitutes one's life or livelihood, the "fruits of the soil" (4:3) that Cain presented to the Lord should under ordinary circumstances have been acceptable to him, because Cain was a man who "worked the soil" (4:2). Even under the rigid sacrificial system of Mosaism, offerings of such plant products as grain and olive oil were not only permissible but also desirable on certain appropriate occasions. To insist that Cain should have brought an animal sacrifice is to read into the text more than is actually there. Hebrews 11:4 stresses the motivation behind rather than the nature of Abel's offering. However correct or costly the sacrifice that a person brings to the Lord, his offering is futile unless founded on faith and undergirded by obedience (1 Sam. 15:22). The attitude of Abel assured his acceptance in the eyes of God because he was motivated "by faith."

Genesis 5 is a chapter of death. The lives of eight preflood patriarchs are described in brief and stereotyped fashion. When

the tally of the years of each life has been completed, we are told
at the close of each paragraph that "he died." The inevitability
of death hangs like a dreadful pall over the entire chapter. We
do, however, catch a glimpse of one sparkling and silvery lining
that breaks through the otherwise unrelieved gloom. Enoch, we
read, "walked with God; then he was no more, because God took
him away" (5:24). His ancestors and his descendants merely
"lived" for a time after the birth of their children, but Enoch
"walked with God" after the birth of his. At the close of their
earthly journeys his ancestors and descendants "died," but Enoch
"was no more, because God took him away." Enoch's firstborn
son, Methuselah, the oldest man in the Bible, thus died while
his father still lived, because Enoch "did not experience death"
(Heb. 11:5). By his life, in his fellowship with God, and through
his translation into the divine presence Enoch became a sterling
example of saving faith that attested him as having pleased the
Lord. Enoch knew, as did Abel before him, that "without faith
it is impossible to please God" (11:6).

The third illustration of faith that the author of Hebrews 11
observed in the Old Testament was that of the patriarch Noah
who, together with his family, survived the flood. Noah is represented as an "heir of the righteousness that comes by faith"
(Heb. 11:7). Himself "a righteous man, blameless among the
people of his time" and one who, like Enoch, "walked with God"
(Gen. 6:9), "Noah found favor in the eyes of the LORD" (6:8)
and "in holy fear built an ark to save his family" (Heb. 11:7).
Noah's confidence and trust in God, however, was not a selfish
faith. He must have labored long and hard to share it with others and to warn them about impending judgment, because the
Bible calls him "a preacher of righteousness" (2 Peter 2:5) who
"condemned the world" (Heb. 11:7), presumably because the
significance of his message and ministry was misunderstood by
his contemporaries. As the ark was being beaten and buffeted
by the waters of the flood, Noah must have praised God often
that he had not earlier in his experience been "blown here and
there by every wind of teaching and by the cunning and crafti-

ness of men in their deceitful scheming" (Eph. 4:14). The Lord in mercy had responded to the faith of his chosen servant.

The author of Hebrews 11 thus selected Abel, Enoch, and Noah as illustrative examples of commendable faith in the earliest periods of human history. These three heroic figures, however, pale into relative insignificance when compared with the next giant of faith that our writer mentions. We are speaking of course of Abraham, whose name is virtually synonymous with the biblical concept of faith. The first explicit Old Testament allusion to faith refers to him: "Abram believed the LORD, and he credited it to him as righteousness" (Gen. 15:6). Whereas Abel received approval from God and whereas Enoch and Noah walked with God, it is said of Abraham that he was the "friend" of God (2 Chron. 20:7; Isa. 41:8; James 2:23). Abraham often talked with the Lord on the most intimate of terms (see Gen. 15:1–9; 18:22–33). While it is true that faith existed before the time of Abraham, it is also true that to be a person who believes is, in a very special sense, to be a child of Abraham (Gal. 3:7).

Hebrews 11 indicates a number of ways in which the faith of Abraham expressed itself. Because his destination was unknown to him, Abraham's migration from Ur through Haran to Canaan was a serious step of faith (11:8). His decision to settle down in Canaan "like a stranger in a foreign country," far from his relatives and friends, is another example of his confidence in God's solemn promises (11:9). The supreme test of Abraham's faith confronted him when God commanded him to sacrifice Isaac as a burnt offering (11:17)—Isaac, who had been born as the result of an earlier act of faith shared by Abraham and Sarah (11:11–12) and through whom the previous promises of numerous descendants were to have been fulfilled (11:18). Although because of his advanced age the potential for parenthood had long since passed him by, Abraham hastened to obey the naked command of the Lord. As far as we know, he had never before heard of an occurrence of a resurrection from the dead, but he believed that God could bring one about if he so desired (11:19). It is because of the prompt obedience that Abraham displayed toward God in response to every divine request (Gen. 12:4; 17:23; 21:14; 22:3) that he can be called the spiritual "father of all who believe" (Rom. 4:11) and that his strong faith compares favorably with that of the Christian in the resurrection of Jesus Christ our Lord (4:23–24).

Three lesser figures from the Book of Genesis follow Abraham as Hebrews 11 continues to list outstanding examples of biblical faith. Abraham's son Isaac blessed Jacob and Esau, Jacob blessed the sons of Joseph, and Joseph spoke about the exodus under Moses (Heb. 11:20–22). Whereas in each case these actions are described as having been made through the promptings of faith, it is clear also that they serve to bridge the gap from Abraham to Moses, because Moses is the second of the two greatest examples of dependence upon God to which the writer wishes to call our attention.

Like Abraham, Moses enjoyed an unusual degree of intimate communion and fellowship with God. We are told that "the LORD would speak to Moses face to face, as a man speaks with his friend" (Exod. 33:11). In his rebuke to Aaron and Miriam because they had spoken against Moses, God reminded them of the clear distinction he made between prophets in general and Moses in particular: "When a prophet of the LORD is among you, I reveal myself to him in visions, I speak to him in dreams. But this is not true of my servant Moses. . . . With him I speak face to face, clearly and not in riddles" (Num. 12:6–8). In a striking passage we learn that the people of Israel sustained a relationship of confidence toward Moses that paralleled their dependence upon God himself: "When the Israelites saw the great power the LORD displayed against the Egyptians, the people feared the LORD and put their trust in him and in Moses his servant" (Exod. 14:31).

Hebrews 11:23–28 enumerates four representative occasions on which faith played an all-important role in Moses' life. As an infant, Moses had been hidden for three months by his parents, who thereby displayed both their confidence in God and their defiance of Pharaoh's edict. As a mature adult, Moses left the

Egyptian court with all its riches and advantages and identified himself with the people of God in all their poverty and persecution. He then left Egypt itself and lived for many years in the land of Midian. Finally he returned to Egypt and, on the eve of the exodus, was instrumental in instituting the Feast of the Passover. In the eyes of the author of Hebrews 11 each of these events was a noteworthy accomplishment of faith.

While it is true that Abraham and Moses shared the privileges as well as the responsibilities of the same divinely revealed religion, it is also true that certain contrasts may be drawn between the faith of Abraham and that of Moses. The faith was basically the same in both cases, but historical and other circumstances caused it to assume somewhat different expressions in the lives of the two men. Abraham was born in Ur of the Chaldeans and thus grew up in a polytheistic household (Josh. 24:2) whose members knew nothing about the one true God. The Lord's call to him, therefore, was unprecedented and earthshaking and absolutely unique to his observation and in his experience, as far as we can tell. Countless Christians who have been converted out of a godless background or environment can sympathize with Abraham and are heirs of his faith.

Moses, on the other hand, was the son of parents who were both members of the tribe of Levi (Exod. 2:1–2). His mother influenced and controlled his formative years and passed on to him religious traditions that had already been developing for centuries. When God addressed Moses, therefore, he could do so in terms that were already familiar to him as a result of his early training and his ancestral heritage: "I am the God of your father, the God of Abraham, the God of Isaac and the God of Jacob" (3:6). Countless Christians who have been converted within the nurture of a godly home and context can sympathize with Moses and are heirs of his faith.

We may also observe other differences between the faith of Abraham and that of Moses, differences that complement rather than contradict one another. Abraham's faith was that of an individual standing entirely alone, while the faith of Moses was that of an individual standing in the midst of a religious community. Abraham was given very few external props to support his faith, whereas Moses performed numerous miracles and experienced many divine interpositions in his behalf. The faith of Abraham was somewhat mystical, but Moses' faith leaned toward ceremonial or liturgical expression. It is important for us to notice differences of this kind because they help us to understand the various directions that modern Christianity, even among evangelicals, has tended to take.

But although its forms could vary, the basic faith remained the same. The Lord knew that Moses would understand when he said to him, "I will bring you into the land I swore with uplifted hand to give to Abraham, to Isaac and to Jacob. I will give it to you as a possession" (Exod. 6:8). God had promised Abraham not only that he would give him a homeland (Gen. 12:1) but also that he would grant to him numerous descendants (12:2) and that all peoples on earth would be blessed through him (12:3). Moses lived to see the provisional fulfillment of the first two of those three great promises, because he led a multitude of Israelites out of Egypt and brought them to the border of the promised land. The faith of Moses and the faith of Abraham were one and the same.

Needless to say, vital trust in the one true God did not cease when Moses died. The chain of faith that had begun to be forged in the life and experience of Abel continued to grow, link by link, beyond Moses and through Rahab (Heb. 11:31), Gideon, Barak, Samson, Jephthah, David, Samuel, and the prophets (11:32)—indeed, down to the heart of a virgin maiden who responded, at first hesitantly and then joyously, to an angelic announcement. Through her was born the Lord Jesus, he who was the final fulfillment of Old Testament messianic prophecy, because "no matter how many promises God has made, they are 'Yes' in Christ" (2 Cor. 1:20). Fastened to a rude cross on a rugged hill outside a rebellious city, Christ became the ultimate object of faith for a dying thief as well as for countless men and women and boys and girls who have since followed in his train. For the contemporaries of Jesus who trusted in him, faith became sight as they joined the ranks of the blessed. To those of us who have accepted Christ since his ascension he says, "Blessed are those who have not seen and yet have believed" (John 20:29).

The all-important master link between that segment of the chain of faith that belonged to Israel and the section that belongs to the church is thus Jesus Christ. God has always asked his children to believe only in what he has revealed of himself and his purposes up to that moment in history in which they live. "Believing God" is the definition of faith that is at once the simplest and most profound. Although they lived in an earlier period and came from an alien perspective, the saints of the Old Testament shared a confidence in God's promises that was remarkably akin to ours. The gallery of the righteous in Hebrews 11 is but a select sample of those who were "commended for their faith" (11:39). Indeed, "the world was not worthy of them" (11:38).

"Therefore, since we are surrounded by such a great cloud of witnesses, let us throw off everything that hinders and the sin that so easily entangles, and let us run with perseverance the race marked out for us. Let us fix our eyes on Jesus, the author and perfecter of our faith" (12:1–2).

10 Redemption

> Return to me, for I have redeemed you.
> Isaiah 44:22

Contrary to popular opinion as held in some quarters, the Bible is not an encyclopedia that gives its readers exhaustive information on every conceivable subject. The Word of God may properly be described as an inexhaustible book only in a certain sense and in limited areas. Its primary concern is to outline God's relationship to us as well as what ought to be our relationship to him and to one another. In the light of this basic understanding of the restricted and specialized nature of the Scriptures it has become quite common in recent years to refer to the main subject matter of the Bible as what the Germans call *Heilsgeschichte*, a term that may be translated literally as "Salvation History" or more idiomatically as "The Story of Redemption." The one true God, the sovereign Creator and Lord of the universe, graciously confirmed his elective purposes for his people by initiating a series of legally defined covenants with them. The theocratic form of government that resulted in Israel was to be made workable by means of a corpus of moral laws that demanded wholehearted obedience and ceremonial ordinances that required sacrificial observance. Israel's basic response to God's boundless provision for his people was to be in the form of an unquestion-

ing faith in him, and the Lord on his part would grant to his
people an unmerited salvation. As a concept that helpfully sums
up the ultimate goal of the biblical narrative from Genesis to
Malachi, redemption deserves a prominent place among the subjects that lie closest to the heart of the Old Testament.

Although intimately related to each other, salvation and
redemption are not simply synonymous terms. Cognate to the
noun *salvation* is the verb *save*, which carries with it the general
idea of deliverance or release from danger, slavery, imprison-
ment, debt, and the like. Cognate to the noun *redemption* is the
verb *redeem*, which connotes the payment of a price by means
of which salvation is effected. Salvation is thus a general concept, whereas redemption is more specific. The redemption price
may be in terms of money, courage, effort, strength, and so on.
In extreme situations the ultimate price, the very life of the
redeemer, is required to achieve salvation.

It is clear that redemption, at least to a certain extent, involves
the idea of substitution that was discussed in chapter 8. To
redeem, one must exchange one valued object for another. The
Suffering Servant of the Lord "poured out his life unto death"
(Isa. 53:12) in order to "justify many" (53:11). Jesus said concerning himself that "the Son of Man did not come to be served,
but to serve, and to give his life as a ransom for many" (Mark
10:45). Christ surrendered his life as a ransom, as a redemption
price, to save the lives of all who would receive him. Paul considered it one of his major tasks to proclaim far and wide the
truth that "the man Christ Jesus . . . gave himself as a ransom
for all" (1 Tim. 2:5–6).

The basis of the redemption terminology found in the Bible
is to be sought in the technical phraseology employed in the law
courts of ancient Israel. For example, one could "redeem" pos-
sessions that had been lost through indebtedness, or one could
"ransom" a needed beast of burden that rightfully belonged to
the Lord. To express the same concept in other terms, under the
Mosaic law it was possible to release either encumbered property or enslaved life simply by making the prescribed payment,

whether in money or in kind. The Old Testament contains many illustrations of redemption in the legal sense, the most pertinent of which we shall now examine.

In ancient times it often happened that a man would find himself so deeply in debt that it became necessary for him to sell part of his property to pay off his obligations. Having freed himself from debt, the man might later wish to buy back his property, especially if he had originally inherited it from his father. Three means of retrieving it were possible (Lev. 25:25–28), only two of which concern us here. He could either redeem it himself by earning enough money to buy it back from its new owner, or his "nearest relative" (25:25) could appear in court and redeem it for him by making the appropriate payment. It should be noted that the latter solution to the problem is preferred by the Book of Leviticus and that only when the impoverished man had "no one to redeem it for him" (25:26) was he to undertake the task of redemption for himself. We should also observe that the privilege, as well as the responsibility, of redeeming lost property always fell to the nearest blood relative.

The story of the marriage of Boaz and Ruth is an excellent example of the way in which such legislation was applied in actual practice. The aged Naomi, the mother of Ruth's deceased husband Mahlon, had decided, for reasons of her own, to sell a parcel of land that had belonged to her own deceased husband Elimelech. In this particular case, with the title to the land went also the obligation of marrying Ruth "in order to maintain the name of the dead with his property" (Ruth 4:5). Since Elimelech and his son Mahlon had already died, and because Ruth herself was childless, and by reason of the fact that inherited property always belonged to the firstborn son, in this case a so-called levirate marriage that hopefully would result in the birth of a male child seems to have been a necessary concomitant of the property sale. The stipulations concerning levirate marriage as they are found in Deuteronomy 25:5–6 are worth quoting in full: "If brothers are living together and one of them dies without a son, his widow must not marry outside the family. Her husband's brother shall take her and marry her and fulfill the duty of a brother-in-law to her. The first son she bears shall carry on the name of the dead brother so that his name will not be blotted out from Israel." If the brother-in-law in question should for some reason refuse to perpetuate his brother's name by deciding not to marry his brother's widow, he would be subjected to public humiliation (25:7–10), and the responsibility of levirate marriage would devolve upon the next closest male relative.

We find a similar situation in the Book of Ruth. When Naomi's nearest relative was told that if he purchased her plot of ground he would also have to marry her daughter-in-law Ruth, he said to Boaz, "I cannot redeem it because I might endanger my own estate. You redeem it yourself. I cannot do it" (Ruth 4:6). Boaz, the next closest male relative (3:12), was thus free to redeem the inheritance of Elimelech and to marry the Moabite woman he had learned to love. We observe again that the redemption of legally encumbered property involved the payment of a price and that in certain instances the means of payment could become quite complex. We must also remember that only a blood relative had the right to redeem in any case.

Situations often arose in which it became necessary to redeem life, whether animal or human. When the Lord inflicted the plague of the firstborn upon the land of Egypt just before the exodus, he spared Israel's firstborn, both man and beast (Exod. 11:4–7). From that time forward, therefore, he would exercise a special claim over "the first offspring of every womb" (13:12) in Israel. Under ordinary circumstances every firstborn animal was to be sacrificed to him in commemoration of his saving grace on that first Passover night (13:15). With respect to animals essential to the livelihood of their owner, however, certain exceptions could be made. For example, because the donkey was an important beast of burden, its master could choose to spare its life by redeeming it with a lamb if he so desired (13:13).

As we already observed in chapter 8, the sacrifice of human life was prohibited in Israel for moral and humane reasons. Nevertheless, since firstborn male children belonged to the Lord, it was therefore necessary to redeem them in some other way (13:13, 15). The divinely ordained means of securing redemption in such cases was to make an appropriate monetary payment. Although merely a token gesture when compared with the priceless value of a human life, the practice was doubtless rigidly enforced.

The account of the redemption of the firstborn found in Numbers 3:39–51 is an instructive example of how such legislation was applied on at least one occasion in ancient Israel. A census of the tribes revealed that "the total number of firstborn males a month old or more, listed by name, was 22,273" (3:43). The Lord decided that the tabernacle service of the Levites would constitute the redemption price for Israel's firstborn males in a carefully tabulated one-for-one relationship. As it turned out, however, there were only 22,000 male Levites "a month old or more" (3:39) by actual count. So it was determined that the extra 273 would be redeemed by having recourse to the above-mentioned monetary payment, which became "the redemption money" (3:46–51).

Redemption of life was also common in an entirely different sphere during the Old Testament period. As a person might have found it necessary to sell some of his property in order to pay off his debts, so also might he have found it necessary, in extreme situations, to sell himself into slavery for the same reason (Lev. 25:47–54). If he was unable to earn enough money to buy back his freedom, a close relative would be obliged to pay for his release. Such examples of legal ransom in ancient Israel stress the concept of redemption as freeing an individual from slavery by means of paying the necessary price. Here also we note that the legal redemption of an enslaved life receives its sanction through its relationship to the exodus experience (25:55).

In point of fact, the exodus of Israel from Egypt constituted the greatest historical act of redemption recorded in the entire Old Testament. As Christians look back with joy to the release from spiritual slavery achieved through the Savior's arms outstretched and blood outpoured, so also did the pious Israelite remember with rejoicing the words of the Lord in Exodus 6:6: "I am the LORD, and I will bring you out from under the yoke of the Egyptians. I will free you from being slaves to them, and I will redeem you with an outstretched arm and with mighty acts of judgment." Needless to say, the redemption wrought by Christ on Calvary was infinitely greater in every respect than the exodus redemption, but we should not permit the differences to so blind us to the similarities that we fail to see that the latter experience typified the former and prepared the way for it.

The name of God that is most closely connected with his redemptive activity is best known to readers of the English Bible as "Jehovah" and is traditionally rendered as "the LORD." That the name "LORD" played an important role in the exodus experience is clear from God's solemn statement to Moses in Exodus 6:2, 3: "I am the LORD. I appeared to Abraham, to Isaac and to Jacob as God Almighty, but by my name the LORD I did not make myself known to them." Since the name "LORD" appears frequently in the Genesis stories of the patriarchs, the aforementioned passage can hardly mean that Abraham and his immediate descendants had no knowledge whatever of it. We should understand it as meaning that they did not know God as Redeemer to the extent that Moses and Israel were about to learn of him. The redemptive context of Exodus 6:2–8 uses the phrase "I am the LORD" no less than four times and thus gives character to the most personal of all the divine names. With much the same emphasis did the later poets and prophets of Israel, especially Isaiah, refer to "the LORD" as the Redeemer of his people (for example Isa. 41:14; 44:6, 24; 47:4).

The redemption of Israel embodied in the exodus expressed itself in two realms, because the slavery of God's people was both external and internal. Israel was doubtless only one among many subject peoples who had been enslaved by the oppressive pharaohs of the New Kingdom period. The political servitude of God's people, however, was more than matched by the harsh and oppressive bondage that they experienced under the cruel taskmasters who forced them to work on the grandiose building projects of the pharaohs. The exodus thus implied redemption from external slavery to the alien power known as Egypt.

But it was not against the Egyptians alone that God and his people were fighting. The war had its internal battlegrounds as well. Although Israel's knowledge of and loyalty to the one true God never died out completely during the 430-year sojourn (Exod. 12:40) in Egypt, the temptation to worship other gods was strong and the Israelites succumbed to it (Josh. 24:14). The bull was a sacred animal in the eyes of the Egyptians. So highly did they venerate it that they deified it, worshiped it as Apis, the bull god, and embalmed particularly fine specimens of it after their death. To this very day visitors to Saqqara, Egypt, may descend into the underground mausoleum known as the Serapeum and examine scores of sarcophagi where the embalmed corpses of bulls were secreted in ancient times. Aaron's observation of the worship of such animals may well have provided him with the idea of fashioning the golden calf to which the Israelites sacrificed in the Desert of Sinai (Exod. 32:1–8). At any rate, the ten plagues that led up to the exodus itself were doubtless intended to demonstrate the fact that the Lord was executing judgment on all the gods of Egypt as well as on the Egyptians themselves (12:12). It may well be that it was by the use of demonic power that Pharaoh's magicians were able to duplicate the first two plagues wrought by God through the agency of Moses and Aaron (7:22; 8:7), but the time finally arrived when the best they could do was to stand back in awe and exclaim to their ruler, "This is the finger of God" (8:19).

Although the exodus experience had been intended as a display of divine redemption for the purpose of freeing Israel from both external and internal slavery, the worship of the golden calf is merely one early example of the countless occasions on which God's people would disobey the stipulations of the Sinaitic covenant. The Israelites usually broke their pledges of loyalty to God almost as soon as they made them. Down through the centuries the Lord found it necessary to punish his people often because of their rebellion against him. The prophets warned them that they would once again be enslaved by foreign powers if they did not repent and cry out to God for mercy. The first three chapters of Hosea, for example, compare the spiritual adultery of Israel to the shameless conduct of Hosea's unfaithful wife Gomer. Because of her brazen wickedness she eventually found herself enslaved to another man. In obedience to God's command, however, Hosea redeemed her from her bondage by paying the appropriate price (Hos. 3:1–2). The subsequent verses in Hosea 3 clearly suggest that God, the "husband" (2:16) of wicked Israel, would in a similar way redeem his people after they had been in exilic bondage for an extended period.

Other Old Testament prophets are even more explicit in their descriptions of Israel's return from exile. Although in a slightly different sense, Micah once again employs the metaphor of a woman in his admonition to Judah: "Writhe in agony, O Daughter of Zion, like a woman in labor, for now you must leave the city to camp in the open field. You will go to Babylon; there you will be rescued. There the LORD will redeem you out of the hand of your enemies" (4:10). Jeremiah, whose predictions of Babylonian exile for Judah are the most daring of all (25:11; 29:10), refers to the Lord as the Redeemer who will plead the cause of his enslaved people (50:33–34). The prophets thus viewed Judah's return from exile as a kind of second exodus. God's oppressed children in foreign servitude, whether Egyptian or Babylonian, cried out for deliverance, and his arm was ever mighty to save.

So far we have treated the subject of redemption in the Old Testament only as it applied to the nation of Israel as a whole. That is the primary emphasis of the sacred writers, probably because of the strong sense of solidarity that permeated ancient civilization in general and Israel in particular. Since clans and tribes were such basic units in the social structure of God's people, they tended to think in terms of corporate responsibility in religious matters also. The story of the sin of Achan in Joshua 7 is a typical case by way of illustration. This is not to say that sin and its resultant punishment were not individual matters as well. From the earliest times God has held the lone sinner accountable for his wicked thoughts and actions, as the story of Cain so clearly demonstrates (Gen. 4:1–16). We are merely attempting to offer an explanation for the relatively few references to individual redemption in the Old Testament. As we might have expected, the poetic literature with its frequent emphasis on personal devotional life provides a rich source for such references.

Self-redemption in any spiritual sense is impossible. A person may have been able to buy his way out of legal indebtedness, but the very idea of self-release from spiritual bondage was repugnant to the Old Testament believer. Only God could redeem (Ps. 49:15), and to that glorious truth the psalmists often gave glad affirmation. The beautiful benediction that concludes Psalm 19 is that of an individual, but it also gives testimony to the belief of Israel as a whole: "May the words of my mouth and the meditation of my heart be pleasing in your sight, O LORD, my Rock and my Redeemer" (19:14). Even in the midst of circumstances that were hardly conducive to praising the Lord, a man whose thoughts were properly attuned to those of the Almighty could staunchly affirm, "I know that my Redeemer lives" (Job 19:25). Fortified with such deathless hope, believers can look forward with supreme confidence to their ultimate release from whatever bondage encompasses them at the moment.

In the New Testament reflections on and developments of the Old Testament concept of redemption, the bondage in view is always and everywhere the demonic power known as sin. Whereas iniquity lies dimly in the background of every ancient form of slavery, Christ and his disciples made it explicitly clear that sin is our real enemy. Intense demonic activity dogged the footsteps of Jesus as he went about preaching and healing. He frequently found it necessary to exorcise evil spirits from the tortured bodies of their hapless victims. The very same Satan who held humankind in thrall had attempted to conquer Christ through temptation at the beginning of his earthly ministry (Matt. 4:1–11; Mark 1:12–13; Luke 4:1–13). But Jesus had emerged victorious over the devil and his minions with the result that, "because he himself suffered when he was tempted, he is able to help those who are being tempted" (Heb. 2:18). When he arose from the grave on the first Easter Sunday morning, he proved that the final slaveholder had been defeated, for death itself could not keep its prey. The resurrection of Jesus guaranteed the ultimate redemption of all who place their faith in him.

Satan and his angels made a remarkable recovery, however, and they are working overtime in the world today. Countless people are still shackled by sin's fetters. All who sin are slaves to sin (John 8:34), and it is Jesus alone who can free them (8:36). But faith is the key that unlocks the chains. Redemption achieved in principle by Christ must become redemption appropriated in practice by the Christian if it is to have any value in personal experience. The gospel is indeed the life-giving and liberating "power of God for . . . salvation," but only "of everyone who believes" (Rom. 1:16). All people everywhere are potentially redeemed, but it is clearly and painfully evident to even the most casual observer that not all people are actually redeemed. Denominational and parachurch leaders, congresses on evangelism, and other mission-minded Christians continue to implore the church to get on with the task of evangelizing the world in our generation. We need to be reminded often of our responsibility to tell everyone we meet that "the wages of sin is death, but the gift of God is eternal life in Christ Jesus our Lord" (6:23). Upon their glad acceptance of the wonderful grace of Jesus they will then be prepared to hear the victorious cry of Paul directed to them as well as to us: "Thanks be to God that, though you used to be slaves to sin, you wholeheartedly obeyed the form of teaching to which you were entrusted. You have been set free from sin and have become slaves to righteousness" (6:17–18).

For Further Reading

Inclusion of a book in the following list does not necessarily indicate wholesale approval of the author's viewpoint or methodology.

Albright, William F. *From the Stone Age to Christianity.* Johns Hopkins, 1957.

Bright, John. *The Authority of the Old Testament.* Abingdon, 1967.

———. *A History of Israel.* 3d ed. Westminster, 1981.

———. *The Kingdom of God.* Abingdon, 1953.

Childs, Brevard S. *Biblical Theology of the Old and New Testaments.* Fortress, 1993.

Eichrodt, Walther. *Theology of the Old Testament.* 2 vols. Westminster, 1961, 1967.

Elwell, Walter A., ed. *Evangelical Dictionary of Biblical Theology.* Baker, 1996.

———. *Evangelical Dictionary of Theology.* Baker, 1984.

Erickson, Millard J. *Christian Theology.* 2d ed. Baker, 1998.

Fuller, Daniel P. *The Unity of the Bible.* Zondervan, 1992.

Hodge, Charles. *Systematic Theology.* 3 vols. Scribner's, 1871; reprint, Eerdmans, 1981.

Kaiser, Walter C., Jr. *Toward an Old Testament Theology.* Zondervan, 1978.

———. *Toward Old Testament Ethics.* Zondervan, 1983.

Kaufmann, Yehezkel. *The Religion of Israel.* University of Chicago, 1960.

Kline, Meredith. *Treaty of the Great King.* Eerdmans, 1963.

Leenhardt, Franz. *Two Biblical Faiths: Protestant and Catholic.* Westminster, 1964.

Martens, Elmer A. *God's Design.* 2d ed. Baker, 1994.

Mendenhall, George. *Law and Covenant in Israel and the Ancient Near East.* Presbyterian Board of Colportage, 1955.

Oehler, Gustave. *Theology of the Old Testament.* Zondervan, n.d.

Ollenburger, Ben C., Elmer A. Martens, and Gerhard F. Hasel, eds. *The Flowering of Old Testament Theology.* Eisenbrauns, 1992.

Pritchard, James B., ed. *The Ancient Near East.* 2 vols. Princeton University Press, 1958, 1975.

Smith, Ralph L. *Old Testament Theology.* Broadman & Holman, 1993.

Terrien, Samuel. *The Elusive Presence.* Harper, 1978.

Thackeray, Henry St. John, trans. *Josephus: The Life* and *Against Apion.* Loeb Classical Library. Harvard University Press, 1926.

von Rad, Gerhard. *Old Testament Theology.* 2 vols. Harper, 1962, 1965.

Vos, Geerhardus. *Biblical Theology.* Eerdmans, 1948.

Vriezen, Th. C. *An Outline of Old Testament Theology.* Branford, 1958.

Wolff, Hans Walter. *Anthropology of the Old Testament.* Fortress, 1974.

Wright, G. Ernest. *God Who Acts.* SCM, 1952.

Subject Index

Scripture Index

118

Scripture Index

Ronald Youngblood is professor of Old Testament and Hebrew at Bethel Seminary San Diego. He has written numerous works, including commentaries on Genesis, Exodus, 1 and 2 Samuel, and Isaiah. He has also edited many volumes, and he was the editor of the *Journal of the Evangelical Theological Society* for twenty-three years.